THE NEW
TERRARIUM

THE NEW
TERRARIUM

Creating Beautiful Displays for Plants and Nature

TOVAH MARTIN

photographs by
KINDRA CLINEFF

CLARKSON POTTER/PUBLISHERS
NEW YORK

Copyright © 2009 by Tovah Martin
Photographs copyright © 2009 by Kindra Clineff

Published in the United States by Clarkson Potter/Publishers,
an imprint of the Crown Publishing Group,
a division of Random House, Inc., New York.
www.crownpublishing.com
www.clarksonpotter.com

Clarkson Potter is a trademark and Potter with colophon
is a registered trademark of Random House, Inc.

Library of Congress Cataloging-in-Publication Data
Martin, Tovah.
   The new terrarium: creating beautiful displays for plants
and nature / Tovah Martin and Kindra Clineff.—1st ed.
      p.   cm.
   Includes index.
1. Glass gardens.   2. Terrariums.   I. Clineff, Kindra.   II. Title.
III. Title: Creating beautiful displays for plants and nature.
SB417.M37   2009
635.9'824—dc22   2008027713

ISBN 978-0-307-40731-3

Printed in China

DESIGN BY MAGGIE HINDERS

10 9 8 7 6 5 4 3

First Edition

To Peter Wooster

CONTENTS

Introduction 9

PART 1

a transparent collaboration: terrariums and you 15

TERRARIUMS DEFINED 16 • TERRARIUMS AND DESIGN 20

NURTURING AND KNOWING NATURE 29

PART 2

the venues 31

COLD FRAMES 32 • LANTERN CLOCHES, OR HAND-GLASSES 35

CLOCHES 36 • WARDIAN CASES 43 • AQUARIUMS 44

BELL JARS, TUREENS, APOTHECARY JARS, AND CANNING JARS 46

OTHER MEANS 46

PART 3

making the case 49

WHERE TO HOST A TERRARIUM 50 • CHOOSING THE PLANTS 55

KNOW THE CASE 60 • DESIGNING THE CASE 61

TOOLS FOR TERRARIUMS 66 • PLANTING THE TERRARIUM 70

PART 4

caring for the case 73

MONITORING 74 • WATERING 75 • FERTILIZING 76 • VENTILATION 78

MAINTENANCE 78 • PATROLLING FOR PROBLEMS 80

PART 5

the plants 83

BEGONIAS 86 • BROMELIADS 89 • CARNIVOROUS PLANTS 90

FERNS 93 • GESNERIADS 97 • MOSSES 100 • ORCHIDS 103

ORNAMENTAL GRASSES 105 • PEPEROMIAS 107 • PILEAS 110

OTHER OPTIONS 112

PART 6

projects 125

A SEASON CAPTURED: SPRING 126 • A SEASON CAPTURED: SUMMER 130

A SEASON CAPTURED: AUTUMN 135 • A SEASON CAPTURED: WINTER 138

COSSETING COLLECTIONS 141 • MEMENTOS 143

A MINIATURE LANDSCAPE 146 • CHILD'S PLAY 150 • MULTIPLICATION 155

RECUPERATION 157

Case Studies 161

Resources 168

Acknowledgments 173

Index 174

INTRODUCTION

THINK ABOUT YOUR NEST. That's right, bring up a mental image of all the elements in your home that you hold dear. Think about your comfort spaces, contemplate the places where the quality time happens with your family and friends, call to mind the time you spend sinking into a soft, cushy chair with shoes kicked off listening to some music, nibbling comfort food, and holding a warm cup of tea. The scene is the epitome of hunkered down, but, to me, it's more soothing when it includes a bit of green.

For as long as I can remember, my life has been tinged with green. Even when I can't escape outside, due to work or the weather, plants and nature are omnipresent. From the moment I first wake up in the morning and find my way past the menagerie of houseplants on the way to the kitchen until the late evening hours when I sit reading, propped up on a mound of pillows beside the fern by my bed, green is my constant companion.

Having nature close makes all the difference. It has colored and calmed my life throughout the most difficult times. Nature has an uncanny ability to spread tranquility wherever it reigns. No matter where you dwell, no matter what you do, there's something about plants and nature that is relaxing. Through calamities, it serves as a touchstone. Through the years, the leaves and fronds of the plants that I've nurtured and the bits of nature that I've brought in to sit by my side have all served to placate and soften the hard, sharp edges of life. If there's one thing I've learned through my life, it is that green is the color of serenity.

And I firmly believe that this is a universality for everyone, wherever they call home. The city might be your setting. And still, you might crave the curative, calming capacity of nature. Perhaps you yearn to take strolls in the park to receive your dose of green. But the park, with its dappled kaleidoscope of colors and soft, leafy shade, is usually just a temporary refuge. Maybe you're hoping to bond with nature when vacation rolls around, but vacation is just a promise in the distant future. Weeks come and weeks go, and still there's no opportunity to escape the pavement and commune with the countryside. What you desperately need is a generous serving of green in your life.

Or maybe you have a home in the country. But your work schedule is brutal, and

Tillandsia argentea adorns a martini glass.

The nature you could never host before, like this masdevallia orchid, can be your companion with a terrarium.

you can hardly find the time to slip out the back door and commune with the meadow down the hill or even link with the patch of lawn outside your door. You hope to feel the pliant give of a forest path underfoot as soon as you can tear yourself away from all the duties that keep you indoors. And yet, the clock ticks away and still you haven't found anything remotely resembling a free moment to connect with your primordial roots. If only it was possible to make that connection—to smell the aromas of the soil and fresh grass, see the earth tones, and return home with a pocketful of acorns, hickory husks, and smooth stones—it would feel so fine.

Terrariums make it possible. Although nature eases life's rough edges, not everyone has time to care for the constant needs of thirsty houseplants.

Botanical endeavors can be therapeutic, but most people lack spare moments to devote to nurturing yet another responsibility. That's where terrariums come in. Terrariums are the tools that can bring plants and people together in a home or work environment with limited effort. They make the close bond between people and nature possible, and they do it strictly on your terms.

Think of all the possibilities. You might spend your days in a cubicle with a computer and a phone for companions. For hours on end you never leave your cramped cubby except for an occasional coffee or to collect the spreadsheets that you printed out down the hall. Sure, there are pictures of your family and your dog within easy glance, but what if there was also a glass bowl filled with mementos from your last vacation? Nothing precious is necessary, just some seashells and some weathered driftwood suffused with a sprinkling of memories. Or imagine something green growing happily in its own little glass case sitting on a pedestal in the corner of that cubicle. Your home office could become a radically altered place if it included a cloche cosseting just a few shreds of birch bark, a pinecone, an autumn leaf or two, and some moss-covered stones gathered from a hike in the mountains. Your workspace could be defined differently if it contained some green, and it would say something about you to everyone who entered your domain.

If you're feeling an ache for the earth but never satisfying that urge, a terrarium might be the solution. Connecting with nature enhances our world, feeds our psyches, stimulates creativity, and—above all—delivers calm. The date you made for tennis or jogging or a concert might be stimulating, but will it change your life? Will it seep into every crevice of your existence, and will it impact you and your family's world? Nature can do all of that. Compared with all the extraneous engagements that bombard your calendar, connecting with green is one of the most important liaisons.

Actually, there's no reason why you've got to make an appointment with nature. It's not necessary to carve out time or leave your space. Nature can meet you halfway. You can't always manage to slip out of your closed quarters—certainly, you can't escape as often as you'd wish—so let nature make the leap to you.

Take a look at the decor in your home. Maybe it's filled with rich

With a cookie jar filled with mosses, ferns, and ivy, an office is transformed by green.

antiques and noble heirloom tables. The upholstery is lush, the colors glowing, and the coffee table is groaning with volumes begging to be picked up and leafed through. Or perhaps the interior of your space is minimal, with sleek contemporary lines and a few sparse but eloquent pieces staged where they'll make the strongest possible statement. Maybe you have some great art on the walls. No matter what your decorating style, having plants coexisting close by with everything else you treasure makes all the difference. Wouldn't it be wonderful if you harbored a little square foot of nature near at all times?

When the weather is foul outside, when you can't manage to leave your children's homework, and when dinner's boiling on the stove, having a plant growing nearby makes all the difference. In the evening after a long, hectic day, it can be incredibly calming to see something from nature happening close to your side. It can transport you to a place where you can lose yourself in the botanical, the blossoming, and the growing. Imagine your home with something green at your elbow, within reach. It sends calming vibes over the scene.

I know that nature has done it for me, but only with the help of terrariums. Wherever I've gone, wherever I've lived, terrariums have come with me. For dozens of years, I've grown plants in terrariums when my environment just wasn't conducive to nurturing plants. When I moved into a place of my own twelve years ago, an antique reproduction wooden terrarium was the first piece of furniture through the door. Since that time, I've planted dozens of terrariums, cloches, bell jars, and anything else glass that would hold plants. Thanks to terrariums, I've always managed to wedge plants into my schedule. My time is as crunched as anyone else's in the modern world and I have precious few spare minutes to spend coddling plants. That's where terrariums come in.

If you live in the city but want to be close to nature, you need a terrarium. If you find yourself in the country but with no time to step outdoors, you need a terrarium. If you are confined to an office fifty hours a week, a terrarium can be your connection with nature. And if your home decor needs a little extra green in it, try a terrarium. Quite simply, terrariums are the solution for bringing all the benefits of botany and you together.

Compose a cloche of twigs, bark, and bits from the wild, and there's no need to put nature on hold while you're working.

a transparent collaboration:
terrariums and you

Your home is filled with beauty and meaning. It's bursting with objects that send your mind's eye floating back to places you've been, cities you've visited, museums you've explored. There's no lack of radiant, bright, splendid moments within the confines of your walls. But does your space include nature?

Look at your surroundings. Do they make you feel an affinity for the Earth, with its woods, wildernesses, thickets, beaches, and backcountry? If you value those aspects of your life, there's a simple way to make them part of your everyday world.

The answer is a conduit between nature and your home. Not only can plants in the traditional sense be yours, but other remnants of nature can also be brought inside to cohabitate. The moss under the tree, the husks of the nuts that the squirrel hasn't stashed, the brightly colored autumn leaves that floated across your path on the way to the post office, the glistening stone that caught your eye—all those treasures could become part of your daily life. And glass makes it possible.

Since early civilizations, people have been employing glass to trick the seasons and secure the fruits of the Earth before their normal time to bear. People have turned to glass when they wanted to frame the outdoors while remaining cozily inside by the fireplace. They've employed glass to bring nature inside and to quench their need to fiddle with flora despite the weather outside. And they've luxuriated in the results. With the help of glass enclosures, enjoying plants is a possibility in places that were previously impossible. When plants are encased in glass, growing goes on autopilot. Tucked inside something crystal and contained, the forest, the beach, and the meadow of your most relaxed leisure moments can merge into (but not mess up) your lifestyle. In glass, the meditation moss that keeps you grounded can sit by your side no matter what the season, despite the time of day or the other commitments in your life. Within a glass setting, it's amazing what some frothy green fern fronds can do.

TERRARIUMS DEFINED

If you've got a dusty image of a terrarium, it's time to update that definition. What we're talking about here is not the stodgy terrariums of your childhood. In recent years, terrariums have taken on a new, sparkling persona that fits comfortably into modern life. These living, breathing bridges between the outdoors and indoors have a new profile that can blend with any lifestyle you happen to embrace. They're sleek, they're sophisticated, and they're current. They make it possible for anyone—gardener and novice alike—to have a green thumb. Think of terrariums as a tool.

So, what is a terrarium and what can a terrarium do for you and your home decor? A terrarium is any transparent confine that allows you to nurture the elements of the green world. In a nutshell, terrariums permit the introduction of nature where nature doesn't naturally reside. The dictionary defines a terrarium as "a sealed transparent globe, etc., containing growing plants." But that's really just the beginning.

Terrariums run the gamut. Delve deep into your recollections of elementary-school science class, and the image you'll come up with when you think of a terrarium is probably an aquarium with a lid. This particular aquarium wasn't devoted to fish—instead, it was holding a menagerie of plants. Maybe it was nurturing subjects for science study, maybe it was just brightening up the biology room, but the teacher had tucked some sort of botanicals inside the glass enclosure. And you might remember that those plants were perking along admirably despite the fact that the janitor paid absolutely no attention to the needs of the botanical collection during Christmas break. That might've been your preliminary brush with terrariums, but even in your formative years and probably subliminally, you gleaned some inkling of what terrariums could do for your life.

Then again, it's possible that your initial mental image of an old-school terrarium is of a clear-plastic soda bottle sawed off and clutching the potatohead plant you just stuck in water, or the marigold seedling that you sowed. Those were the typical elementary-school introductions to the concept. But all this has changed. As the years have passed, you've undoubtedly encountered terrariums in many different guises, from glass cloches to miniature greenhouses that could easily sit on a side table or stand on their own pedestal. Terrariums are more beautiful than you might remember from the past. They've gained character and dimension; they are no longer only defined by what they nurture inside. They now have scope, significance, and a presence as design elements. Not only do they nurture plants, but they also add beauty to your home's decor. Terrariums have become incredibly diverse.

Terrariums are almost always made of glass, clear plastic, or acrylic, but that might be the only trait they share. Terrariums can be dome-shaped cloches with a knob for lifting; they can be shaped like a greenhouse, or something more elaborate. A terrarium can be a glass vase with a plant tucked inside it, or it might be a Mason jar holding a faux clutch of robin's eggs or the remains of the long-ago-deceased dragonfly you found on your dashboard. A terrarium might be the cold frame where you keep your tomato plants in the spring or the hotcaps that you clamp over the melons to make certain they don't freeze. Some terrariums have spent their former lives holding goldfish, others are wide-mouthed glass bowls meant to serve grapes or fruit compote. They can be candy jars or lidded cheese plates, beakers or test tubes given a second career. Everything is open to interpretation, and the glass you have at home might be begging to be recycled into a terrarium. For its first job, an antique glass battery case might have put in long hours doing useful service of a very mundane kind, but during its semiretirement, that battery case might serve the function of bringing nature into a drab interior world.

More important than their physical traits is the fact that terrariums all create a certain set of conditions that make bringing nature inside possible, even in the most unfriendly conditions. That's where terrariums have had a critical influence on our lives. What a dictionary can't define is the far reaches of a terrarium's impact. A terrarium opens the possibility

ABOVE A mini-cloche can be a terrarium; this one holds a newly propagated begonia plantlet.
OPPOSITE As beautiful as any artistic masterpiece, an etched-glass jar recycled into a terrarium cradles *Chirita longganensis.*

for plant life to survive where it never managed to dwell before. In that capacity, terrariums have become invaluable tools.

A terrarium truly is a small world. Terrariums with plants serve as tiny biospheres. When they nurture plants, terrariums become mini-environments that provide an atmosphere of elevated humidity for all the botanical contents that they embrace. If a terrarium is a sealed case (and not all terrariums are necessarily sealed cases—some have ventilation, some have unfixed panes, some are open at the mouth or side), it acts as a closed ecological system, with an ongoing cycle of moisture evaporating from the soil and the natural ingredients inside. That moisture wicks up through the soil to eventually produce condensation within, continually moistening the soil and atmosphere. The plants survive, photosynthesizing and creating oxygen just as they would function in the great outdoors. They chug along, going about their life processes, but their daily existence is spent in a small, contained space.

Not all terrariums are completely sealed, but the humidity is still elevated for the begonia inside this unfixed, paned Wardian case.

When you close a sealed glass case with a plant sequestered inside, within minutes condensation starts building up on the glass. That's the biosphere beginning to work its magic. That's the exchange of vital forces revving up. The opaque quality of a steamy case, with water droplets dribbling down and the plants inside partly obscured behind the sweating panes, is part of its romance. It's also a sign that a small world is progressing as it should.

Not all terrariums are sealed, and they don't all cloud up with moisture. But even a glass vase with an open mouth elevates humidity levels slightly and helps plants to survive in homes that might not be conducive for nurturing nature. Tuck a plant into anything glass or plastic and enclosed, and it will glean similar benefits. This goes far beyond that simple closed transparent globe that you might remember from childhood. The possibilities are vast.

TERRARIUMS AND DESIGN

When you imagine nature indoors, you probably think of houseplants. And the houseplants that cross your path might not fill you with either euphoria or inspiration. If you're looking for nature, you're probably not

finding it in the plant section at the grocery store. What you see in the supermarket houseplant-wise is rarely striking in a design sense, and it isn't apt to start anyone's creative juices flowing. The overall presentation is sorry, to put it mildly. First of all, everything is anchored in plastic. And those plastic pots tend to be manufactured in the least complimentary shade of leprechaun green imaginable. Basically, the container clashes with the foliage. Nothing would inspire you to adopt that plant since it has no resemblance whatsoever to nature as you know it. But if you repot it and put it in a terrarium, you've surmounted your first aesthetic obstacle.

Given some flare, houseplants are certainly salvageable. With a little shine, they can be redefined. In fact, they have tremendous potential to uplift your daily life, especially when some chic is instilled into their look. And why not? Why can't houseplants gather a whole new persona that befits the glow of your sparkling kitchen? Why couldn't the colors in the accessories of a room's decor be emphasized by some punchy little plants? There's no reason why you can't reinvent houseplants and integrate them as an element of style. A houseplant face-lift, an update, and a style check are all within the realm of possibility. The nature that you want to live with is at your fingertips with a terrarium.

What could offset a fledgling begonia as smartly as a curvaceous apothecary jar? Using seashells as an underpinning stashes souvenirs from the beach as well.

Try rethinking what you're given and try perceiving it through unbiased eyes. This isn't about that dowdy little cyclamen in the plastic pot looking so forlorn in front of the city florist, it's about what you could make of that cyclamen. Approach even the most mundane African violet from a creative angle, and it's redeemed. This is like recycling. Give a plant a sleek surrounding, and the polish is transferred to its image.

It's also possible and not so difficult (thanks to the Web, but also if you haunt your local garden center) to search beyond the ordinary. Start by finding plants that you want to live with. Choose plants that you find personable. Don't accept only what's readily at hand. Look far and wide. Experiment. There's a vast world out there and it's filled with treasures. When you seek beauty, it's amazing what you find.

Terrariums can be implements in a makeover. When glass enclosures enter the scene, not only is gardening possible inside your home, it's downright glamorous. The ante is upped as far as aesthetics go. You've elevated houseplants to an art form. Everything speaks to a heightened

The Ethics of Wild Plants

A LITTLE discussion of woodland ethics is appropriate here. Wildflowers should be protected; I'm not suggesting that you go out and reduce native populations of wildflowers in order to fill your terrarium. Consult nature for inspiration, and then go shopping. Many woodland plants—in fact, most wildflowers—are available in containers from nurseries that grow and propagate them specifically to increase the bounty and to sell to the public. Adopting a nursery-propagated wildling and nurturing it under your wing is a truly good deed for the environment. It's the best tactic to take. The last thing you want to do is deplete nature, and you definitely won't be curtailing stores of wildflowers if you buy from a reputable source that propagates its own plants. Even such woodlanders as partridgeberry and cushion moss, as well as rarities such as pitcher plants, can be acquired from nurseries. There's no need—or excuse—to gather these precious plants from the wild.

And, to be honest, it's difficult to dig a wildflower and see it survive. Because they're not grown in a contained space, the roots of wild plants tend to wander and travel deep into the soil. The odds are slight that you'll successfully gather what you need below ground to secure a favorable outcome. Chances are that the soil will fall away as you dig because wilderness soils don't have the same makeup as potting soils. And a plant with exposed roots is in a precarious situation. It's tricky for the experts. For a novice, it's nearly impossible. Even in a terrarium, it's easier to go with a plant that's been previously grown in a container.

But if you have the expertise to access nature, please obey all the rules of collecting. Don't do it if you don't know the territory. Learn what is scarce and what is prolific. Definitely learn more about the endangered plants in your region. And, although a plant may not technically be endangered, it might be unwise to collect it from the wild. For example, many mosses are extremely slow growing and should never be taken from the wild. They may not be endangered, but they have a fragile existence. Instead, purchase cultivated, farmed moss. It's readily available. Similarly, princess

pine is beautiful and highly desirable. But it's not an easily renewable resource. Go the nursery-grown route.

If you feel confident collecting a plant that you know for sure is prolific and appears in large colonies, the safest, most conscientious approach is to take only a tiny sampling and leave the bulk in place. Obey the same rules that guide any sort of wildflower collection. Leave natural ecosystems with plenty of fodder. Avoid removing plants that are on the verge of dispersing seeds; wait until after they've scattered their progeny. And never collect from parks, forests, or nature preserves. Similarly, your neighbors might not be thrilled if they find you with a trowel digging away on their property. Again, your safest bet is to buy plants from a nursery.

Rather than collecting in the wild, purchase native ferns that have been propagated in a nursery.

perception that runs parallel with the sensibilities you put into gear when furnishing your house. You can play with the relationship of nature, terra-cotta, and glass and let textures complement one another. With glass as part of the idiom, the wheels are set in motion for something totally unique to transpire.

So, where can you go now that you're adding terrariums into the plant/interior equation? Glass enables all sorts of options. The garden center might sell a heuchera for the perennial bed, but there's no reason why you couldn't have it in your apartment. It might fit into the ambiance perfectly, with the help of glass. There's no need to settle in with the tried and true. You can experiment with different plants that you've always

LEFT Smarter than knickknacks and less apt to gather dust, ferns and mosses in jars infuse green into any decor. **ABOVE** Crowning a cakestand, a plant under a cloche imparts instant sparkle.

RIGHT Offset in a glass cube, orchids get the framing they deserve. OPPOSITE This may be the only way you'll ever be able to introduce an ornamental grass into your office space.

wanted to nurture—perennials, ground covers, orchids, bog plants, carnivorous plants, whatever—and substitute them for houseplants. Every environment is different. Every room is its own microcosm. And every eye sees things differently. Bring all those stimuli together, and you've got the makings of something uniquely personal.

So, there's no need to confine yourself to what we traditionally think of as houseplants. You can go even wilder. Although they might not be on the beaten path, many woodlanders and shade-loving wildflowers are appropriate for terrariums. Plants that you pass by during hikes and walks might be perfectly willing to settle comfortably into glass and become part of your habitat. Here's where you might have the closest bond; these plants might be the ones most meaningful to you. It's entirely possible to fill a crystal kingdom with plants like the ones encountered when you were last outward bound.

Terrariums on the Job

MERGING PLANTS into the workplace is easier than you might imagine. Even if you have space constrictions (and space is always an issue in the office), a plant can take just a few inches of tabletop if it's in a jar or a compact terrarium. It doesn't need to monopolize your desk, and a terrarium also lets you focus on your work rather than the needs of its occupants. Bottom line is, you've got an object that will bring a breath of fresh air into your cubicle with a minimal amount of work.

If your workspace includes access to a window, you're home free. Even if that window faces north or has light obstructions from other adjacent buildings or trees, you can nurture mosses, ferns, or ivies in its near proximity. Brighter windows can host plants that require more light, but you should monitor the incoming rays for their intensity. Direct sunbeams can cause burning inside a closed glass case. Surprisingly, autumn light sometimes comes streaming in particularly intensely due to the low angle of the sun coupled with the sudden loss of deciduous tree canopy during that season. By the time winter rolls around, the light typically isn't strong enough to cause any problems. However, if you're working in certain parts of the country, your windows will act like summer, no matter what the time of year. A good rule of thumb at any time might be that if you have to squint against the sun, it would be wise to pull a terrarium away from the panes. Or at least keep an eye on it for signs of burning leaf tips.

Of course, not all offices have the benefit of windows. Fortunately, you can still nurture plants in a terrarium. Houseplants have been known to survive solely on incandescent light, especially low-light-loving terrarium plants. It's certainly worth a try. And before you begin supplementing light, you should attempt a terrarium with the light that is available. Even desk lamps might nurture an African violet and coax it into bloom. Often you can move a terrarium to a strategic spot that is sufficiently close to the existing fluorescent tubes to make the setting work for a terrarium.

Positioning the terrarium is the key. Needless to say, the closer a plant dwells to its artificial light source, the more light it will reap. Glass terrariums can be posi-

tioned as close as a foot (but no closer) from fluorescent tubes, but such intimacy might not be necessary for most low-light terrarium plants. Experiment with the distance. However, always avoid potential fire/burning risks and take care not to place terrariums or plants too close to bulbs and fixtures, especially if you're working with a light source that can produce heat or terrariums made of materials such as plastics or acrylic.

Light is virtually all you'll need to furnish for a terrarium. The terrarium itself will be responsible for the rest of a plant's requirements. If your workspace is unpleasantly dry, you needn't worry, because the terrarium elevates humidity. You can go on business trips galore without needing anyone to plant-sit. When you return to the job, your terrarium will still be perking along.

And there is no need to discount plants that are difficult (like orchids), or plants that are so small they're generally overlooked. Glass is a facilitator; it creates a conducive environment for plants that would never survive inside. But it's also an enhancing agent. Glass can sharpen the image, or soften it, depending on the setting. It will imbue anything within its confines with a totally different feeling. Changing the context is what terrariums are really all about. More than merely enabling tools, they're uplifting. No matter how mousy, give a tiny little plant a crystal kingdom of its own, and it will shine.

NURTURING AND KNOWING NATURE

Think of the terrarium as a tool. Terrariums are like full-time assistants, saving time, sharing chores, shouldering responsibilities, expanding your realm. Glass diminishes the thirst of anything contained inside. Part of the benefit of the biosphere action is that humidity is held within the closed environment, keeping the contents evenly moist. So, rather than the dry/wet cycle that usually results when you invite plants to live indoors, this is a constantly moist situation. Not all plants like that sort of treatment. But those plants that do grow luxuriantly. The venue is stress-free, and plants respond.

From a purely practical standpoint, terrariums reduce the number of times you have to visit the faucet. But the elevated humidity also has other perks beyond the benefits of keeping the soil evenly moist. The reason why orchids are perceived with fear and trembling by anyone who doesn't have a greenhouse at their disposal is because orchids demand high humidity. And the average home's climate is often compared to the Sahara desert. If you've suffered from chapped lips, static shocks, and a dry throat, especially during the heating season, the culprit is probably low humidity levels. Your house may be dry, but a terrarium solves this problem for whatever sits inside. Terrariums are like greenhouses, in scaled-down versions. They're tabletop humidity chambers. And again, plants thrive as a result.

ABOVE Snowdrop blossoms won't last long in a terrarium, but they're worth the brief thrill. **OPPOSITE** With a tendency to shed, *Pilea macrophylla* would make a messy roommate, but it's under wraps within glass.

the venues

Terrarums take on all sorts of guises; they come in many forms. More than being a set of physical characteristics, a terrarium creates a specific set of conditions for whatever is being sequestered inside, and the concept was certainly not born yesterday. Since people began putting spade to soil, terrariums have been employed to help in the process of growing. In that capacity, they have acquired many shapes and configurations, depending on the functions they performed and the region where they were used. Although there are extremely elaborate terrariums available, they are only a sampling of a gardening tool that has inspired the handiwork of craftspeople and laborers alike. And despite the fact that terrariums currently have a thoroughly modern demeanor, they have deep roots.

COLD FRAMES

Although they're not the picture that immediately comes to mind when you bring up a mental image of a terrarium, cold frames are the most primitive mode of sequestering plants in glass cases. They generally dwell outdoors. But the beauty of it is, cold frames can be used indoors and translated into a modern home setting. It's not the obvious application. But think about it: Anytime you use a display case to exhibit your shell collection, anytime you adopt any sort of box with a glass lid to shelter the remains of butterflies that fluttered onto your windowsill and perished, you're working with a descendant of a cold frame. Call them display cases if you will, it's the same theory.

Cold frames are cited as the direct grandparents of the technology that became greenhouses. Granted, they were the most primitive version, but the theory is there. Basically, a cold frame is just a rectangular box with a translucent lid. It could be wood, it might be metal, it could be an open-bottomed frame, or it might be solid beneath. In the traditional sense and for gardening purposes, cold frames are employed outdoors to protect tender crops from the cold. Often a cold frame is nothing more than a set of windows straddling a slanted box—the windows shed light on whatever is confined within. Although heating units aren't a part of the picture, the sunbeams (keeping in mind that outdoors is where cold frames traditionally dwell, and they're typically positioned in the sun) warm the residents while the solar rays simultaneously encourage the growth of everything within. What you're doing is harnessing solar energy to force the seasons.

Anything shielded within a cold frame is kept snug when the temperatures plummet and then given fresh air as the mercury rises. With that description in mind, the window overlay is generally hinged so it can be lifted and set ajar, allowing the fresh air to cool whatever is growing inside. There's not much headroom. And due to those height restrictions, what's inside is usually fledgling. After seedlings germinate, when they're on their way to reaching sufficient maturity to be planted in the garden but still aren't ready to go it alone, they're placed in cold frames. The same is true for cuttings and small, newly purchased plants. For that purpose, the cold frame serves as a halfway house of sorts. It hardens

ABOVE AND OPPOSITE Although display cases aren't technically cold frames, they're ideal for exhibiting treasures. **PREVIOUS PAGE** Terrariums come in many shapes and sizes; almost any glass enclosure can function as a terrarium.

Hand-Glasses in History

ALTHOUGH THEY were probably in use by the 1600s, it wasn't until glassmaking processes improved and glass became less expensive in the 1820s that hand-glasses (also called lantern cloches) were readily available. Meanwhile, it was the province of nineteenth-century garden writers to extol their virtues and put them in the common domain. Lantern cloches found their champion in the British writer J. C. (John Claudius) Loudon. In his early-nineteenth-century classic *Encyclopedia of Gardening* (1822), he urged the gardening world to avail itself of hand-glasses, his favorite being dome-shaped and made of copper and glass. Lead was cheaper, but not as elegant. The cast-iron two-part version, the base being polygonal, the lid being pyramidal, was also highly recommended. But he made his message clear— "the essential utensils of gardening are the sieve, flowerpot, watering-pot, and hand-glass."

His wife, Jane Loudon, took up the crusade with her gender, while also describing the common use of this tool in *Gardening for Ladies* (1849), suggesting that "every lady should have two or three hand-glasses, of different sizes, always at her disposal, even during the summer, for the convenience of sheltering newly transplanted plants."

off seedlings to the chilly, cruel world after they've been coddled in the relative warmth and coziness that hastened sprouting, rooting, or propagation.

That's the typical definition of a cold frame, but shrink your concept of cold frames down, bring it into your abode, and you might have a venue for one of your many collections.

ABOVE Antique lantern cloches can be found at flea markets and garage sales, but the lids have often lost their partnering base.

OPPOSITE A lantern cloche can be as simple as a four-sided base with a pyramid dome.

LANTERN CLOCHES, OR HAND-GLASSES

The term *hand-glass* isn't often used today. Nowadays, this particular glass-paned object might be called a lantern cloche or miniature greenhouse. But *hand-glass* was the original term for this heavy-duty, many-paned, portable, pyramid-shaped box made to fit over individual plants. Think of the lantern roof light that you sometimes see at the tops of buildings in the city, shrink it to about 2 feet square, and you've got a very close cousin. Plus, all sorts of shapes and configurations came into being, from octagons and many-paned domes to contraptions that looked like large portable cold frames. The square, cast-iron version of the lantern cloche is the one that you most often find in British antique shops; that was the medium that survived due to its substantial craftsmanship. Copper versions were considered to be more upscale, although not as prolific or durable. But lantern cloches aren't only antiques. You can easily snag a new reproduction that appears deceptively similar to the original nineteenth-century cast-iron heirlooms, and at a very reasonable price.

Although lantern cloches were sometimes single units, the two-part type is most easily manipulated. In the case of the two-part type, the base is made of four glass panels screwed together into a square, and it's meant to remain in place. Above that base is the pyramid top, which can be clamped tightly on, set askew to allow fresh air's entry, or lifted off entirely. For growing purposes, the easy aeration is incredibly convenient.

Lantern cloches work with a variety of plants. Because they were traditionally set directly on the soil over melons or some other tender crop, they have no floor. As with cold frames, straw was originally used to insulate beneath (beware of this tradition—when used outdoors, it's an open invitation to nibbling rodents). Take the same tool, switch its surroundings to indoors, and you have an eloquent accent, and the tool remains fully functional. Fitted over potted plants with saucers to catch any excess moisture and perhaps a zinc tray and cork pad under it all to protect the furniture, a lantern cloche can serve as a terrarium.

CLOCHES

Basically, a cloche is a large glass dome, made to be clamped over plants in inhospitably chilly weather. Unlike a lantern cloche, which has individual glazed panes, a cloche is one curvaceous solid-glass unit. Envision an oversize glass bell (the British sometimes called them bell-glasses) and you've conjured a fitting mental image.

Protecting plants from a chill was a cloche's earliest function. Whole

Cloches come in all sizes, ranging from one large enough to sequester an orchid to a pint-size version nurturing a peperomia cutting.

fields of tender melons, tender violets, lettuce, and other crops in need of cosseting were once sheltered under cloches when the weather was inclement. But, of course, we now have plastic versions—called hotcaps—to do that job much less expensively and with no fear of breakage. The cloche's hardworking days are over, but its inherent beauty keeps this tool in vogue for a whole different purpose. No longer workhorses outdoors, cloches are treasured primarily for their charm.

Cloches are a blissful marriage between a tool with a purpose and a graceful piece of art, a rare combination in the agricultural world, which might explain their staying power over the centuries. They're an open invitation (okay, a closed invitation) to create something truly sparkling. Because the parameters are prescribed, and because they're scaled down to manageable proportions, cloches offer the ideal forum for setting a small stage.

Whether you use them practically or decoratively, cloches have an Old World splendor. They come in all sizes and shapes, from tall and slender to wide and stout. Of all the types of terrariums available, the simple, unfussy lines of a cloche make it an interior design tool with finesse and roots. Plus, cloches no longer cost a mint. Reproduction cloches are omnipresent nowadays, so there's no reason to seek out or spend a fortune for an antique version. New models are readily available with all the singular imperfections and gray-green tinge of old thick bottle glass. Some are flared at the base, like a bell; others are straight-sided or gently curved inward, like an inverted cup. And they generally have a knob on top for easy manipulation. When cloches were used in the field, that knob came in handy when weather permitted or the sun demanded that the cloche be removed or cracked ajar (generally bricks, stones, or pieces of wood are enlisted to ventilate a cloche). However, if you can find an antique version, the knob is often broken off, and that missing knob has become part of the legends surrounding garden antiques. Some would say that it was knocked off intentionally to avoid the magnification of the sunbeams that the knob caused. Others claim that the absence of knobs is merely a casualty of continually handling the glass, especially due to shipping. As one antique dealer put it, "It makes a good story, but it's probably just clumsiness." Knob or no, if you use a cloche indoors out of danger from direct or overhead sun, the magnification issue is not a factor.

Hosting an orchid and poised to be a centerpiece, a cloche imbues its inhabitants with a sense of importance.

Wardian Cases in History

NATHANIEL WARD never planned to set the world on fire. Changing the botanical scene as he knew it was probably furthest from his mind when the surgeon went on a country ramble one sparkling day in 1830 and slipped a hawk-moth pupa into a glass bottle. As he plugged the cork, undoubtedly just for safekeeping or force of habit, little did Dr. Ward imagine that his whim would trip a series of events altering horticulture forevermore.

Back in London, Dr. Ward in all likelihood forgot the sealed bottle for several months. It was out of sight, out of mind for half a year. When he happened upon it again and checked his pupa's progress, what had transpired in the interim must have come as somewhat of a surprise. The chrysalis had made no headway whatsoever. But a fern had sprouted.

To be specific, the fern that sprouted in Ward's case was *Dryopteris filix-mas,* the male fern, rock-solid hardy (USDA Zone 4 in the United States), and a very common occurrence in the cool, moist woods of Europe (as well as in North America). It's a handsome fern, with lance-shaped, deeply segmented, waving fronds. But what caught Dr. Ward's attention was not the fern itself. To the contrary, the male fern isn't any sort of rarity. What hit the surgeon/amateur naturalist was the fact that a voluntary sporeling plus a tuft of grass had appeared totally unbidden, and were thriving in London with no intervention whatsoever from him. Having struggled to perform the fern-hosting feat for years, he finally had a salubrious fern growing indoors without effort. The fact that he hadn't raised a finger to cultivate the contents didn't escape the good doctor. He hadn't watered, misted, or otherwise fussed over the enclosed plants in six long months. Not only was this hands-off gardening at its finest, but it had legs.

The discovery might have sparked only passing comment from anybody else. But Nathaniel Ward published his findings, and he presented the scientific paper in 1841 before an expert and esteemed group of listeners, with an enthusiastic reception. As a result, Ward began designing more-elaborate glass cases. And the buzz began.

Apparently, the world was just waiting for this sort of diversion. By 1851, the original bottle—with its incumbent fern still chugging along on autopilot—was displayed at the first world's fair, held in London. The little prototypical biosphere was one of the many curiosities profiled in the Crystal Palace, the glass enclosure where the exhibition was held. From there, the concept of a sealed environment to coddle plants took off.

To claim that the Wardian case, as it became known, changed the world isn't exaggeration. At first, the case was just a closed glazed box—rectangular in shape, glass on all sides, looking like someone shrank a greenhouse. Gardeners adopted that case, and all its ramifications, for purposes of gardening indoors. Ferns were a favorite, hardy ferns being the only possibility at the time. But tropical plants also eventually became potential players, thanks to the Wardian case.

Explorers were simultaneously beginning to search the world for treasures of all types, and every expedition had a botanist aboard. Prior to Wardian cases, collecting sprees were confined solely to retrieving seeds and herbarium specimens due to the length of the sea voyage on the return trip. As anyone who has ever traveled with plants will attest, it's a trial to keep living things in a live state during transit. And the problems were compounded by the fact that ship hands were loath to share precious freshwater rations with plants. One dose of salt water, and whatever plant happened to be on deck was history. Few plants survived.

That changed with the introduction of Wardian cases. Conveniently fitted with handles for easy maneuvering, the self-contained cases (closed also to sea storms) went on expeditions and returned filled with salubrious plants that required no fuss or water during their journey. By and large, if the plants were happy in the jungle, they were equally content in closed cases. As a result, plants from rare orchids to elaborate tropical ferns managed to make it safely back to Europe. Eventually, those tropical plants were within the realm of indoor gardeners—thanks to Wardian cases.

Immensely popular with the Victorians, Wardian cases are back in vogue.

WARDIAN CASES

You've probably encountered a Wardian case, but didn't know precisely what it was called (or what to do with it). A Wardian case is a glass- (or glasslike plastic or acrylic) enclosed house. Wardian cases often look like miniature greenhouses with all the ornate embellishments associated with those glass houses. But that's not the only configuration. Wardian cases can be as simple as a rectangular glass box with a lid, or they can be astoundingly intricate. They've been designed to imitate famous architecture throughout the world, as well as mimicking in miniature many of the better-known public British greenhouses. They might sit on a tabletop or be freestanding; the freestanding types frequently have the importance, craftsmanship, and components of fine furniture. Some are taller than they are wide; others have side wings or cupolas. Even the smallest Wardian case is at least 6 inches or longer, and they're at least 6 inches high at the peak. That's space just begging to be filled.

A Wardian case (without moss or anything that might produce moisture) can serve simply and elegantly as a display box for a collection of anything small—from a group of toys to a rock garden. Or it might furnish a place where you house a collection of shells. Originally, Wardian cases cosseted ferns, but there's no reason why you can't use begonias, orchids, peperomias, or whatever works, mixing and matching at whim.

One factor to consider is whether your Wardian case has ventilation, which is nothing more complex than a door or lid that might be swung open or propped ajar. Versions with ventilation are the most practical. The airflow inside can be adjusted to suit your specific home environment.

Interestingly, few truly antique cases have survived into the present. Perhaps because they were made of breakable components, they didn't stand the test of time. Except for a few rare examples, all that remains are innumerable engravings of what was once a rampant fad. But no matter. Modern versions of the Wardian case do a fine job of mimicking the originals. There's scarcely a style that hasn't been reproduced sturdily to endure wear and tear. They remain the Rolls-Royces of terrariums.

Often built to replicate a house or greenhouse, benches and all, a Wardian case can be incredibly ornate.

AQUARIUMS

Cloches and Wardian cases are the mainstream for terrariums, it's true. But this concept can be expanded. In fact, it can be redefined. For those with ingenuity, there's always the less traveled road. And if you generally take a novel approach, then you're apt to find something that will do the same job as a store-bought terrarium, recycling what you've got on hand. In a pinch, aquariums perform the same function as a terrarium. They're watertight, and leakage won't be an issue when you water the plants.

Why not convert the dusty bowl that once housed your goldfish into a terrarium? Granted, you'll have to fill most aquariums with plants that remain compact, but that leaves plenty of options. Cover the top with a pane of glass, and you've got a closed environment with high humidity. Leave it lidless, and you can host plants that don't want or need close quarters as far as the atmosphere is concerned.

ABOVE Even when open, an aquarium raises the humidity for what grows within. **RIGHT** The fish bowl that once harbored guppies can nurture a begonia instead.

Or move the aquarium concept into larger digs. Go beyond the gold-fish bowl. Aquariums come in all sizes and can nurture just about anything you hanker to have in your home. Fill one with water, and aquatic plants are an option. Or fill the aquarium's floor with soil and grow plants. Again, a lid will raise the humidity while also putting a cap on the height of the incumbents. An open aquarium still increases the ambient humidity, but plants can pop over the edge. And don't discount the usefulness of a cracked or leaky aquarium stored in the basement or snagged at a yard sale. With some sort of tray underneath (copper is one option, but there are plenty of cheaper ways to go, including plastic trays), it can hold soil. Or leave the plants in their containers with saucers underneath. Either way, you'll be watering the plants less often than plants grown in the open air.

A covered tureen can be enlisted to cosset groundcovers.

BELL JARS, TUREENS, APOTHECARY JARS, AND CANNING JARS

In the sleek and streamlined department, bell jars and apothecary jars predominate. They are sometimes footed, but not always. They can be either straight-sided or bowl-shaped, with or without a lid. Whatever shape they come in, bell jars, glass tureens, and apothecary jars can certainly be recruited for terrarium duty. They're available in a broad range of sizes, and the more voluminous versions have the potential to sequester several plants. But even modest apothecary jars can be conscripted.

Canning jars can also be used and the theory is the same. They come in all sizes, with clear or lightly colored glass. As long as it isn't dark and doesn't exclude light, colored glass works for terrarium plants that prefer dense shade. And canning jars can be used with or without their lids. Minus the lid, they aren't as steamy as the closed versions, but as long as a plant is cradled in glass, the humidity will be increased.

In a long, slender moss-filled vase, a paphiopedilum orchid sends up blooming spikes.

OTHER MEANS

The sky is the limit as far as terrariums are concerned. Any glass vessel can and should be enlisted; there are no restrictions. As long as you can make a venue work, you're free to tinker with anything from glass flower vases to wineglasses. Powder jars, water pitchers, cookie jars, goblets, globes, and battery cases are all apropos. You could even use a glass curio cabinet as a terrarium venue in a pinch. Or you could enlist glass beakers, test tubes, and laboratory flasks. Not everything needs to be airtight. Open-mouthed glass items can be a way to go. As long as you can fit the plant inside, you're free to make it work. And if you can't fit a plant inside without inflicting fatal damage to its foliage, put in some soil and try a seed.

Stretch your ingenuity. Why not use a hurricane lamp or a lantern as a terrarium? Hurricane lamps are just waiting to hold something other than a candle. They generally have a door for easy access, and have ventilation at the top. They come in all sizes and styles, they're readily available, and, after all, they need a job in wintertime. But these are just a few ideas. Look around the house and you'll find plenty of potential terrariums.

making the case

IF YOU'VE NEVER DABBLED IN THE DIRT BEFORE, A TERRARIUM IS THE PERFECT PLACE TO TEST THE WATERS. IN THE PAST, YOU might have been all "brown thumbs" when it came to houseplants, but this is different. With the aid of glass, terrariums are a much more forgiving venue than a windowsill. Making one is not difficult, even if you're not a gardener. Of course, the more you learn about the details of doing this right, the more apt you'll be to secure success.

First of all, consider how you'll be using your terrarium. Most often, terrariums are used as a permanent mode of growing plants in the home. The goal is long-term care, and terrariums are planted purposefully with the future in mind. In that case, you'll want to carefully follow instructions to help your terrarium survive over the long haul.

However, not all terrariums are meant to last. Some terrariums are composed like flower arrangements, good for just a brief stint of glory. If the goal is merely to exhibit something in a cloche or terrarium for a temporary interlude—say, for the duration of a summer's picnic, or an evening's event—there's no reason to worry about the process. The foundation can be composed of whatever you need as a base, no sweat. No urgent need to worry about the details and add pebbles, charcoal, and so on. Just make a momentary scene happen and bask in the compliments.

In the event that a lingering relationship is on the horizon, if you want that terrarium to take you through the winter or longer, that's when careful, thoughtful planting with the proper components will make the difference between a terrarium that survives without intervention and something that needs fiddling and replanting. With a terrarium, the foundation is everything. What you do up front can make a major difference down the road.

WHERE TO HOST A TERRARIUM

Before you adopt any living thing, your first thoughts should focus on where you'll entertain your new acquisition, and plants are no exception. Outdoors, it's easy—just find room in a bed depending on whether the plant wants sun or shade, moist soil or dry earth. Indoors, placement is also not difficult. But thinking about location will ease this little bit of nature into your life and decor.

So, your first task is to become familiar with your home. Think about your living space in relationship to plants. Do a quick survey of the windows and light sources available and monitor the movement of light through your home. The availability of light might surprise you. Even during the darkest days of winter, light pockets might stream through and certain areas might be bright even though they aren't directly in windows.

Your heating situation isn't as critical as it would be if you were growing plants out in the open without the benefit of a terrarium. However, it is necessary to avoid radiators when they are in use and spewing hot air during the heating season. And unheated attached porches are dangerous when frosts hit. But besides those two extremes, terrariums protect plants from fluctuations in temperatures—that's one of their traditional applications.

The suggestions here are aimed at terrariums with plants. If your case is filled with nonplant treasures from the forest—in other words, inanimate objects—then it's not necessary to concern yourself with the details of positioning in relation to light sources, and so on. But even if your terrarium has one small fern, you should consider its well-being and cultivation preferences.

Hosting Considerations

TERRARIUMS with plants should be positioned:

- **IN CLOSE PROXIMITY TO A LIGHT SOURCE:** Any terrarium that's cradling plants will need some light. Even mosses require light to survive. And that's where most people err with terrariums. They tuck them into a dark and dreary corner. Instead, give yours the benefit of a window, fluorescent lights, or some other light source.

- **IN INDIRECT LIGHT:** Some light is critical, but too much light can be a killer. In most environments, an east- or west-facing window in winter is an ideal habitat for a terrarium. Even a north-facing window will work if it receives ample light and depending on what you're growing.

- **AWAY FROM DIRECT SUNBEAMS:** This is a rule that applies across the board. No matter what you're growing, bright, direct sun doesn't jive with a terrarium. Any living thing grown within glass can potentially scorch in hot, direct sun. The glass magnifies sun. Plus, heat builds up in the closed quarters—think of a car with the windows shut on a hot, sunny summer's day, and you've got a fitting analogy. Pull your terrarium away from direct sun. But also keep in mind that the sun moves with the seasons and the influx of sunbeams alters when deciduous tree canopies lose their leaves.

- **UNDER FLUORESCENT LIGHTS:** If using artificial lights, be sure to use lights that are designed for growing plants, obeying and considering all safety precautions. And follow the recommendations for the use of fluorescent lights with plants, positioning the light source sufficiently close to allow the plants to benefit but not burn. Take care when positioning lights beside plastic and acrylic terrariums, as they can melt.

- **INDOORS, OR IN A SHADY OUTDOOR VENUE:** Again, planted terrariums won't do well in sun, and bright light is difficult to monitor outside. Unless you've got an outdoor location where shade is always available, keep your terrarium safely inside.

- **IN A HEATED ROOM:** Cloches were originally used to protect plants from a light frost. And they still perform that function, but only to a certain extent. A cloche will not protect a plant from hard frost. When temperatures go down below 30°F, the contents of a terrarium might be in danger of freezing. Not only is that the case outside, but it's possible indoors on an unheated porch or breezeway, or in a mudroom as well. Don't take the risk.

- **AWAY FROM A HEAT SOURCE:** You don't want to bake the contents of a terrarium. Don't sit a terrarium on a radiator that's spewing forth heat. During the heating season, it's best to keep a terrarium away from an active heat source. An air-conditioning unit can also be a wild card. Central air shouldn't be a problem, but a window-installed unit blowing cold air directly on a terrarium might not be a good pairing.

- **AWAY FROM SUDDEN EXTREMES IN TEMPERATURE:** You're working with glass, after all. Sudden fluctuations in temperature can be the death of a cloche, not to mention its inhabitants. Treat cloches the same way you would handle any glass container.

- **AWAY FROM FINE FURNITURE:** Rather than risking damage to fine furniture or carpets, don't put a terrarium on or above a surface that could be ruined. And always use a tray beneath. Even terrariums that appear to be watertight aren't always reliable, and the moisture from a humid case can cause staining or mold; put some sort of protection beneath.

Maidenhair ferns detest direct sun, so tucking them away from a window and in a terrarium is optimal.

CHOOSING THE PLANTS

What works in a terrarium? Again, anything can survive inside a glass case temporarily. If you've got an event and want to put a zonal-leaved geranium in full flower or some other plant that loves and needs bright light into a terrarium for the evening, by all means go for the glitz. And remember to take that plant out of the terrarium after the party is over. But if you're hoping for a longer haul, it's best to find plants with certain characteristics and cultural preferences that make them prime candidates for life in a terrarium. Some plants are custom-made for terrariums (see suggestions in Part 5, starting on page 83, but that's just the beginning). Here are the criteria.

- **SMALL WORKS BEST:** The easiest route is to find miniatures that remain mini. Sure, it's possible to install plants that are diminutive now but will ultimately get larger. But who wants to replant a terrarium when something is doing well? When you work with miniature plants, monitoring progress won't be a constant chore. And there will be no need to worry that the plant will outgrow its home.

- **SHADE-LOVING PLANTS ARE IDEAL:** Since a terrarium can magnify light, the best plants to grow are botanicals that prefer and perform in a shady environment. And that works for several reasons—when a sun-loving plant doesn't receive sufficient light, it is stressed. And the last thing you want to do is stress your plants. Right?

- **PLANTS TOLERANT OF HIGH HUMIDITY ARE THE TICKET:** A terrarium tends to get moist, especially if it's a closed case. Select plants that are fond of that sort of environment. Humidity-loving plants are usually native to the rain forests of the world, but that isn't always the case. Woodland plants also tend to do well, portraying a more familiar native look. Avoid plants that hail from arid regions. Few Mediterranean herbs can survive in a terrarium. The same is true for cacti, succulents, and most alpines—they don't tolerate the elevated moisture levels.

If you're generally a brave, adventuresome sort of person, you may be willing to jump right into a terrarium filled with that rare and expensive orchid of your dreams. And you might have beginner's luck. It might succeed like nothing you've ever tried before. But to be wiser you could test the waters with something easy and economical.

With the double protection of a saucer and cork, a little chirita won't harm the wood surface below.

RIGHT Ferns, especially compact ferns such as this *Nephrolepis cordifolia* 'Duffii', thrive on the elevated humidity afforded by glass. OPPOSITE Even if your home lacks humidity in winter, orchids, begonias, and ferns are within your reach given a terrarium.

Not only is small better as far as finding suitable plants, but, just as you might suspect, it's generally easiest to work with plants that are in small pots rather than larger containers.

Where can you find diminutive plants? Often it's possible to obtain small plugs of plants (this can be a little deceptive—all plants in plugs are small when they start out, but like Great Danes, they can eventually get big). So, when you get a plant in a plug, research the ultimate size if you're planning a permanent display rather than a temporary scene. Even more readily available are plants in 2¹/₂- to 3-inch pots; they're also ideal for planting in a Wardian case or base of a cloche. In addition to selecting plants that are diminutive in growth, pick ones whose root systems are also compact.

You'll have two options when planting inside a terrarium:

OPPOSITE: Even if your home lacks humidity, winter orchids, begonias, and ferns are within your realm, given a terrarium.

1. You can purchase a plant in a pot that can fit inside your terrarium, or transplant into a pot that fits inside.

2. Or you can remove the plant from its container and transplant directly into the soil of the terrarium.

To a certain extent, you can manipulate root systems to fit into your venue. Ground covers, for example, typically send down shallow roots. Although they might be in a deep container, most of the soil underneath is not penetrated by the roots—skim it off to make the plant fit your purposes. Other plants are also apropos, if their root system isn't too expansive. However, keep in mind that too much ripping and tearing of a root system can lead to transplant shock. Don't be brutal. Although you're giving a plant the ideal environment in which to recover, a wilted plant might not impart the dazzling impression of your dreams immediately, especially if your terrarium is bound to be the centerpiece of a party.

LEFT When in doubt, ask about the mature size of a fern before containing it in a terrarium—this *Polypodium fallax* remains sufficiently compact. **OPPOSITE** Dig a snowdrop, bring it indoors, plant it in a pot, and enclose it in glass. When it fades, you can bring it back outside.

KNOW THE CASE

All sorts of different terrariums are available. Some have ventilation, some do not. And terrariums provide different levels of humidity, depending on their design and construction. Here's a list of different venues with the most humid environments presented first and moving down to terrariums providing less humid conditions.

- A cloche provides the most humidity. When you clamp that bell over a plant, it's in a closed environment and humidity will collect inside if there's any soil at all as part of the configuration. Although a cloche is one solid unit, ventilation is possible if you use something to allow air to flow when necessary (I use terra-cotta "feet" for raising pots off the ground).

- A lantern cloche will also have high humidity if the glass is glazed into the frame. However, lantern cloches usually offer the possibility of ventilating when necessary. If a lantern cloche is composed of two units, it can be ventilated by setting the lid askew.

- A bell jar or apothecary jar with a lid becomes a closed, humid environment when the lid is affixed. Or it can be ventilated by lifting the lid or setting the lid akimbo.

- A closed Wardian case can also be a sealed environment if the glass is glazed into the frame. The easiest sealed-paned Wardian cases to work with have ventilation of some sort rather than a solid piece that fits over the base.

- Wardian cases are available with inset glass panes that can be lifted out of hinges in the frame. These are not closed environments and require more attention to watering than is necessary in a sealed cloche or case. But they have the benefit of allowing you to grow plants that don't need or want very high humidity.

- Aquariums can be open, or they can be fitted with a piece of glass to close the top. Tanks often have wide open mouths; fish bowls have smaller openings. Humidity will vary depending on the size of the aquarium's mouth.

- Vases, tureens, and compotes generally have open mouths. Humidity within will be higher than a plant grown in the open air of a room with no glass enclosure whatsoever. Surrounded by glass,

Given its sealed panes, the miniature world inside this Wardian case should chug along with little intervention needed from you.

humidity from the soil lingers slightly. But the humidity level will not equal the high moisture in a cloche, for example. An open vase, tureen, or compote requires occasional care—you'll need to water once a week or so. But still, ministrations are minimized.

DESIGNING THE CASE

Design is simple—it's the balance of shapes, textures, and colors. It might be pithy, it could be crisp, or maybe it's discrete. You have the option of going soft and flowing, whimsical, or bizarre. As a rule, expressing your-self with strong, clean, sharply defined, articulate objects is a perfect game plan. That's why a miniature obelisk gives the exclamation point that directs your eye and makes you notice its companion plants. The goal is to turn attention to what is not usually noticed, and because a terrarium enthrones whatever is contained within, you're already halfway there.

Plant combinations can also play into the yin/yang principle. The way to make all botanical elements of a scene eye-catching from a textural standpoint is to work opposites. Opposites (or complements, if you will) are always effective. If you've got a fluffy moss, why not bounce something shiny off it? If a begonia is a nebulous mass of leaves on long stems, give it definition by coupling it with an item that possesses solid, strong lines. Or the electrifying component could be a container with a punchy glaze. The container that you choose for accompaniment isn't everything, but it's of the utmost importance. If you're working with a mini impatiens and its pot matches or complements the hues in the plant's foliage or the shades in a petal, all the better. Sometimes it's about texture or shape. An urn balancing a cloche can look smartly sophisticated or it might be rustic, depending on whether you've chosen cast iron or weathered terracotta. Match the look with your decor and taste.

Color can be a feature as well. This is where the patterns in leaves take on a new prominence, especially if you interplay the markings in more than one plant. Again, complements accentuate features. If you've got a begonia with dark foliage, sit it beside something chartreuse. Or if everything in your terrarium is dark, punch it up with a brightly colored bloomer—a flowering orchid is perfect. Because terrariums generally dwell in the shade, luminous elements always add to the composition. White takes on new meaning in a terrarium.

When your composition has several elements, give each space to shine. Don't crowd a terrarium. Of course, there's something meaningful about a plant striving for freedom from a terrarium—a few stray branches poking out is poetic, without a doubt. But the container shouldn't appear crammed. It needs breathing room. On a purely practical level, the foliage needs space, or it will begin to suffer from fungal problems.

Collect promising elements beforehand, and be selective. Planting in odd numbers tends to fill space easily, especially when you're working with something that's round—such as a cloche. It's helpful to think in patterns. Have you ever noticed that a threesome is an easy combination to contrive? Plus, if your terrarium is being lit from only one direction—if

To add a bright spot within this giant apothecary jar, a porcelain cabbage holds a tuft of dyed moss.

LEFT To play off a fern, select something with shiny leaves and flowers, like this codonanthe. Then add a ground cover, such as this pilea. OPPOSITE Just as in designing a garden, combine plants of different textures and related colors in a terrarium.

it's sitting in a window, for example—a trio of plants looks good from all angles, allowing you to rotate it periodically so that all facets bask in balanced light. Diversity is easy to achieve with three plants—you can use an upright plant sitting beside something that forms a mound, and then juxtapose that duo against a ground cover to create harmony. If your terrarium has room for more than just three ingredients, an easy way to expand is to continue working in threes. For each upright constituent, find a creeping ground cover and a rounded, mounding companion as well. This provides a straightforward formula for increasing numbers without becoming bewildered.

Working from the middle outward is also an approach that works, especially on a round stage. Your focal point and tallest object (whether it is a plant or a statue, or whatever) should sit toward the middle—which is also commonly the highest part of a terrarium. From there, work outward.

Think about vistas, too. Just like gardens frame settings, the interior of a terrarium needs to be visible. Since you'll want to show it off from all angles, be sure that the view in isn't obstructed by tall objects blocking sight lines. And be ready to clip plants back if they begin to overstep their boundaries and encroach on their green neighbors. Above all, feel free to have a lark. What you're creating might be a small world, but it has the potential to make a major statement.

TOOLS FOR TERRARIUMS

Depending on which type of terrarium you're targeting and what you plan to grow inside, you'll be using different ingredients for putting your terrarium together. Some of these ingredients, such as soil and pebbles, go pretty much across the board. Others are variable depending on the requirements of the terrarium you plan to plant and how fancy you want to get.

When working with terrariums, have on hand charcoal, potting soil, pebbles, a watering can, moss, and gloves.

- **POTTING SOIL:** By all means, use your favorite potting soil—as long as it isn't too muddy. How do you test that? Easy—just take a handful of the slightly moistened potting soil in your hand and make a fist. Then open your hand. If the soil clumps together in a ball, it probably needs more sand and peat moss. If it falls apart when you open your fist, it's perfect. If you don't have a favorite mix, then opt for something that isn't heavy and offers plenty of drainage. If it has a generous helping of sphagnum moss and peat moss in its configuration, all the better. No need to mix your own soil. Store-bought soil mixes work fine.
- **PEBBLES OR GRAVEL:** Pebbles or gravel can provide two services. They can furnish drainage below the soil and they can top-dress the soil to make a clean scene at ground level. Actually, there's a third function that pebbles provide—you can spread them on the soil surface and create paths to mimic walkways in an inner-terrarium garden or roads through a mini town. For topdressing, use any stone size you favor (or none at all—this is optional) for the look you're creating. For drainage, you want tiny $1/4$-inch pebbles or smaller gravel—larger stones might be handsome, but they aren't a good idea.

Water tends to percolate down and collect at the bottom, requiring occasional drainage, which can be messy.

- CHARCOAL: Whenever you're planting a terrarium, it's wise to use charcoal. Activated charcoal pieces (not grill briquettes), often sold as an aquarium supply but also found at garden centers, serve to filter the water, sweeten the soil, and prevent stagnation and fungi that can accompany lack of drainage. Whenever a container has no drainage hole, charcoal is the way to go.

- **SHEET MOSS:** Moss is more than just an ornamental feature in a terrarium, although it definitely serves to set the stage for plantings. One way to wick water away from plant roots is to line the bottom of a container with moss. It works particularly well with bell jars and glass-bottomed containers; the texture adds a visually compelling element seen through the glass beyond just the brown of soil. And it virtually sponges up excess water.

- **GLOVES:** In the safety realm, you'll want to wear gloves when working in the soil and also when working with moss. When handling sphagnum moss, there's a danger of being exposed to a fungal infection called *Sporotrichum schenkii,* a serious affliction affecting the skin. Therefore care should always be taken not to come in unprotected contact—wear long sleeves as well as gloves. Gloves are also essential when handling charcoal.

- **TROWELS:** This tool is certainly not a necessity. But you can sometimes score a mini trowel at an antique sale that is the perfect size for working within a terrarium. Long-handled tools are also convenient.

- **MISCELLANEOUS OTHER TOOLS:** Long-handled barber's scissors might come in handy. Or a mini rake to clean up the soil could prove useful. If you're working with sand or pebbles, a pint-size rake is particularly helpful. In case you need to tamp down the soil around a newly inserted plant or firm a cutting into the soil, try

making your own terrarium tool from a bamboo stake or barbecue skewer with a wine cork stuck onto the tip. Long-handled, blunt-nosed tweezers also prove helpful for shifting things around if you can't get your hand through the opening of a terrarium. Experiment with long-handled salad tongs—they might make your work a breeze.

- FUN INGREDIENTS: Anything is game when filling a terrarium. As long as you don't combine something that rusts or is ruined by moisture with plants, moss, and soil (moisture is inevitable in a planted terrarium), then the sky is the limit. Color-fast is good when it comes to gnomes and the like. Find or make mini trellises. Hunt up any sort of minuscule ornaments that you favor. Dollhouse furniture (if it won't be harmed by moisture) is certainly appropriate. Or go totally natural and profile stones, nuts, seeds, leaves, pods, and whatnot from the woods. This is the fun part.

PLANTING THE TERRARIUM

Now that you've got what it takes, you can get started with the actual planting. And really, thinking a terrarium through and getting all the ingredients amassed is more than half the battle. The actual planting is fairly straightforward. After you've tried it once, you'll be throwing terrariums together with the greatest of ease.

There are all sorts of terrariums available, in a variety of shapes and sizes. Not all have a base that can accommodate plants tucked directly inside. If the base won't hold water or isn't sufficiently deep to hold plants, opt for growing a plant in a container placed inside. For terrariums with a base that can be planted, there's a general series of steps that work no matter what type of terrarium you plan to plant. There are several variations, for sure (see Case Studies, starting on page 161), but this is the general process. And, fortunately, it's fairly simple. Here's what you want to do:

Start with a clean terrarium. If your terrarium or aquarium has been used previously, be sure to wash it thoroughly and disinfect if necessary. Always wash out any disinfecting products and air out the terrarium completely for several days before adding new living things. Bleach can harm plant roots if they come in contact with it.

Mix a generous handful of charcoal with your pebbles and lay a bed of that mixture in the bottom of the terrarium. If the base of the terrarium is sufficiently deep, lay a level layer of an inch or so of this mixture.

Next, add a layer of soil. The thickness of the soil layer depends on the depth of your terrarium base and the plants you plan to insert. But generally speaking, if you are working with plants in plugs or 3-inch pots, 2 to 3 inches of soil should suffice. Tamp it down lightly to diminish air pockets and level it.

If you're working with plants with a deeper root ball going into a shallow base, you can lightly shake some of the soil free and tease the roots out horizontally. One trick that's often used is to slit the root ball down the middle and pull out both halves horizontally. Try to inflict minimal damage on the small, water-drinking rootlets around the outer edge of the root ball. They serve as the wicks to drink water.

Dig little pockets in the soil for inserting the plants. Just like planting

When planting a vigorous root system in a shallow base, slit the root ball and pull the halves out horizontally.

a garden, it's wise to leave plenty of room between neighboring plants if you're going for a grouped planting.

Insert the plants in the pockets, making certain that all the roots (but not the plant stems or crowns) are buried in soil. Exposed roots will eventually dry out, leading to wilting and a weakened plant.

Firm the soil around the newly transplanted plants. Again, this is a step that you don't want to leave out. No need to cement the plant into its bed, but it's imperative that no air pockets remain around the roots. A cork on a barbecue skewer is a useful tool toward this end.

Water lightly—very lightly. You're adding moisture to get the ecosystem within started. What you don't want is muddy, waterlogged soil.

Add any ornamental extras that you'd like, such as twigs, stones, leaves—or gnomes!

Close your terrarium and watch it grow.

caring for the case

THE BEAUTY OF TERRARIUMS IS THAT THEY REQUIRE MINIMAL LONG-TERM CARE. WHEN IT COMES TO MAINTENANCE, terrariums are pretty much trouble-free if they were planted properly. But that said, terrariums should be monitored for signs of trouble. And every once in a while, you might need to step in and provide some water or disentangle a couple of plants that are overstepping their bounds. In all probability, intervention will be necessary much less frequently than the care required for houseplants growing in the open. Plus, if the need to intercede occurs, it's apt to be a thoroughly enjoyable experience.

RIGHT The mini palms (actually palm seedlings) in this ornate little crystal palace were planted in tiny urns to create the look of a small world. OPPOSITE TOP Clean glass gives a sharper view on what's going on inside a cloche. OPPOSITE BOTTOM Watering the terrarium won't be a constant chore, but it might be occasionally necessary. PREVIOUS PAGE A Wardian case with a deep base simplifies planting directly in the case.

MONITORING

Keep an eye on your terrarium, even under optimal conditions indoors. Although opening the lid continually might throw off the rhythm of the ecosystem, you can easily check things out by peering through the glass at your small world. The beauty of terrariums is that you can see what's going on inside. While you're enjoying your little, confined scene, take the opportunity to make sure that nothing is wilted, that mold isn't growing, and that all the plants are cohabitating in harmony. Occasionally, your assistance might be needed. Act immediately when you see trouble brewing—preventive action can save a situation from flaring out of hand, necessitating the replanting of the whole terrarium. Mold can spread like a plague. Nip it in the bud. Remove it immediately by covering the infestation completely with a cloth or paper towel to contain any spores. Keep the towel closed until it's away from all plants, and then toss it safely in the garbage. Then remove any weakened stems nearby (and the entire plant if necessary) that might be a hotbed for future problems. With vigilance, your small world can continue working its magic.

WATERING

The whole theory behind a terrarium is to eliminate or reduce the amount of watering that the plants inside require. This is as close as nature comes to autopilot. In a closed bell jar or sealed Wardian case, watering might not be necessary for months at a time. But you still want to monitor the situation. Inspect the contents, make sure that nothing is dry, and check to see if the soil inside is slightly moist. Wilting is never a good sign—but it can signal too much moisture as well as insufficient water. Try to ascertain where the problem lies. If possible, intervene before a plant begins to look faint. And in the event that a drink must be furnished, do it lightly. Never drench the contents of a terrarium.

Although it would be nice to be able to say definitively "once a week" or "twice a month" to explain how often water should be given, nothing in nature follows an absolutely regular, predictable schedule. The thirst of the plants in a terrarium varies according to the type of terrarium, the weather outside (whether it's sunny or cloudy, or whatever), the amount of light provided, the type of heat, the temperature, and so forth. All those variables affect how often supplemental water must be served. And all those factors alter with the seasons. Water might not be required at all throughout a dreary autumn. You could go for weeks or months without carrying a watering can. However, in summer, watering once a week might be necessary. Monitoring the occupants is the only way to judge when water is needed.

When a case or jar is open, it will probably require occasional water. In most instances, the amount of water needed will be far less than for plants that aren't cosseted in glass. The frequency of watering depends on the plants in the terrarium. Large ornamental grasses, for example, are heavy drinkers wherever they grow. And certain aquatic plants just slurp up the moisture, even when grown in glass jars. Other plants will probably only demand water on an infrequent basis.

Water should be given when the soil inside begins to become dry. When in doubt, open the case and feel the soil by inserting a finger to test its moisture content. When planting in sheet moss, this can be difficult to judge, but sheet moss should look sparkling green and appear slightly moist. Never wait until the soil or moss is parched or "bone-dry." At that juncture, the growing medium usually fails to take up moisture and water simply runs down the sides of the terrarium to its bottom.

The important factor is to water sparingly, especially if a terrarium has no drainage. A small drink will probably do the job and introduce moisture into the environment. If you're growing in moss, be particularly cautious—moss holds water; all that's necessary is enough water to moisten the moss surrounding the plant. Soggy is never good. And, if you must err, goof on the side of less rather than more water.

When the moss in a terrarium is sparkling green, it's a telltale sign that it's sufficiently moist inside.

FERTILIZING

A chore that you can virtually cross off your to-do list is fertilizing. Terrariums really don't need fertilizer. After all, the goal is to keep the plants diminutive and extra food would beef them up in a counterproductive way. Since you're watering the plants minimally or not at all, fertilizer salts might build up. I've never fertilized my terrariums, and they just chug along beautifully. Given the low light conditions that terrariums prefer, and considering that you're trying to keep the plants within in check and discourage rampant growth, feeding just doesn't seem necessary, especially in a closed terrarium. However, if you've got an open vase or aquarium and the foliage of the plants inside begins to turn pale, by all means, give them some food. If you go that route, dilute the fertilizer liberally.

VENTILATION

Knowing when to introduce air into the terrarium can be tricky. Theoretically, a terrarium should be able to survive for months, even years, without fresh air. However, sometimes mold enters. In that instance, it's wise to let a little fresh air rush in (after removing the offending schmutz). If the plants inside are losing leaves, that's another indication that fresh air might be necessary (or that the plants in the terrarium aren't suited to the environment).

When you ventilate a closed terrarium, do it judiciously and briefly. Rather than taking the top off, first open a window or ventilator in the case. Rather than removing a cloche completely, set it up on something (again, terra-cotta "feet" work well for this purpose). Give it a day or a few days to breathe. During that time, remember to water the plants inside—plants housed in a terrarium can make lush, lax growth that quickly wilts when a closed environment is suddenly exposed to the elements. Then give the terrarium another drink, if necessary, before closing it up again to get the biosphere action happening.

MAINTENANCE

Again, this is nature, and you're hosting it—so occasional intervention is necessary, to the benefit of the contents and your edification as well. Although terrariums are generally self-sufficient, it might be necessary to step in occasionally to make sure that everything goes like clockwork.

The more often you inspect a terrarium, the better. Most of the time, you'll just come away with a vague sense of joy from having encountered nature's bounty. But sometimes you'll need to take action.

When plants are happy, they grow. And terrariums can delight plants to the point that they outgrow their quarters. A plant can only survive for so long with its leaves pressing against glass. When something outgrows a terrarium, it should be graduated, plain and simple. You could lift the overgrown plant and give it a larger terrarium, you might divide it and replant half into another container, or you could remove it entirely and start again with something small.

Even dwarf plants require grooming to remain suitable in size for an apothecary jar.

Similarly, it's not wise to let plants vie against one another in a limited space. When those tiny plants grow larger and begin to flex their muscles and compete for space, somebody's got to go. If you don't intervene when plants begin to brawl, you're apt to lose everything. Instead, divide or prune back plants.

It's critical to keep a terrarium clean. Any yellowed or damaged leaves or plant parts should be removed immediately. Flowers are lovely while they happen, but the moment they begin to fade, they should be whisked away. Anything that's deteriorating will court fungal and bacterial infections. It's an accident waiting to happen.

Keep the glass clean. Obviously, you want a spotless window on your small world. But it's not only about making everything dust-, smudge-, and fingerprint-free. You also need to wipe off any smut or debris from the inside of the glass to prevent disease infestations.

To make sure that all sides of a terrarium are illuminated equally, rotate the terrarium occasionally. This is particularly helpful when light is coming from only one angle. If the plants farthest from the light source are stretching or bending toward the light, rotating will even out light distribution.

PATROLLING FOR PROBLEMS

Theoretically, a closed terrarium shouldn't be prone to insect infestations. After all, it's sealed off from the world. Of course, if a plant enters paradise with eggs or "wildlife" on its leaves or in its soil, then an infestation can quickly get out of hand. Purchase plants from a reputable source, and check your plants carefully for evidence of insects before putting them inside a terrarium. A quarantined observation

period is not a bad idea. Look for the telltale signs of red spider mites (a netting of tiny yellow dots on the underside of the foliage, and fine webs), check for aphids (succulent little critters that vaguely resemble ants), look for scale (little brown bumps on the leaves), and examine your plants for anything that resembles an egg case on both the tops and undersides of leaves, as well as stems. Checking with a magnifying glass isn't being overly cautious—it's just being practical. And if you find an infestation, don't risk contaminating the whole mini neighborhood. Discard, or at least quarantine, the infected plant.

Occasionally, snails and slugs can climb into a terrarium. After all, it's their ideal habitat—moist and shaded. Although you might think they're sort of cute at first, don't let them remain. You can't imagine how much damage those slow-moving, leaf-chewing critters can do in a very brief amount of time.

Fungal and bacterial problems are the main issues that plague terrariums. Unfortunately, they can spread rapidly and knock out an entire plant population in no time. Generally, healthy plants will not fall victim. But just like the common cold can run rampant in a nursery school, fungus can also attack previously healthy plants when it gets started. Prevention is your best weapon. Keep the terrarium clean, don't crowd plants, and grow plants that are meant to be hosted in a terrarium. In particular, select plants that prefer low light levels. When a plant that requires sun is deprived, it will become stressed. And a stressed plant is more likely to develop problems.

Of course, one use of a terrarium is as a convalescent unit for ailing plants. If you use your terrarium to heal the sick, segregate those plants. Don't try to mingle the healthy with the ill. And if you begin to lose the healing battle, discard the plant. And then disinfect the terrarium.

If a problem occurs, or when you're replanting a terrarium, clean it up completely. Never recycle moss, soil, or other organic ingredients from terrarium to terrarium. Start fresh. And when you're using household cleaners on the interior of a glass case, rinse and air the case out completely for several days before refilling it.

You can't be too careful. And all the extra attention you lavish on a terrarium will show. You want to keep a terrarium as sparkling as the rest of your home.

Segregating plants in individual terrariums (or, in this case, hurricane lamps) can serve as an initial quarantine period.

the plants

ONCE YOU'VE EMBRACED THE TERRARIUM CONCEPT, YOU NEED TO THINK ABOUT THE SPECIFICS. HERE'S WHERE your personal taste in plants matters most. Many plants are apropos; the challenge is to find something that speaks to your sensibilities, or quenches a dream. Take this opportunity to grow an orchid or an air plant that you've always yearned to host. For a terrarium to be truly relevant—for it to be all that it can be—find fillers with a connection. Think it through, let it percolate, give your creative juices a chance to mingle—this is art, after all—and then begin to play.

A few ground rules will get you going in the right direction. First of all, selecting good bedfellows is imperative. You want plants that will play well together—that's the primary criterion. And you need plants that will thrive.

RIGHT Although *Muehlenbeckia complexa*, the maidenhair vine, doesn't boast showy flowers, in a hurricane lamp it turns a workspace around. **OPPOSITE** Low-light-loving *Saxifraga stolonifera* doesn't demand the humidity of a lantern cloche, but the setting transforms it into a conversation piece. **PREVIOUS PAGE** Native to Tasmania, *Viola hederacea* wouldn't be a hardy violet outdoors, but it thrives inside in a terrarium.

Start out by knowing the playing field. Not everything works in a terrarium—in fact, appropriate plants tend to share certain traits. Because it's dangerous for a terrarium to sit in direct sun, shade-loving plants are particularly suitable. The exception would be when you stretch the definition of terrariums to include open, wide-mouthed bowls, glass compotes, or tureens. In those instances, because heat isn't building up, you can safely work with sun lovers. But when a terrarium is closed or nearly closed, shade is the safest way to go. And the shady environment infers certain limitations. Foliage plants are the obvious avenue. Terrariums teach an appreciation for the subtle nuances in leaves, texture, and stature. If flowers are your objective, your options aren't as many, but there are ample possibilities. You could go for an orchid. Try a member of the African violet family, a begonia, a mini impatiens, a Hawaiian heather, or a violet (especially the profuse-blooming Tasmanian violet, *Viola hederacea*).

Terrariums also provide high humidity, so appropriate plants to bring into closed cases prefer a moist atmosphere. Any glass enclosure will raise

THE PLANTS   85

the moisture level in its immediate surroundings, even if the top is open. Make that work in your favor—exotic plants that you could never host before are now within your realm. Think of a terrarium as an enabling tool toward making all your dream plantings into possibilities.

Think small. Remember that you're working within a finite space. If you choose plants that are naturally petite, you'll be able to keep them contained for a long-standing stint. A permanent relationship can be yours. The bigger guys aren't out of your reach, but a heftier enclosure will be necessary to accommodate their girth. Plus, let's face it—part of the beauty of a terrarium is the "small world" aspect. At a time when everything tends to be larger than life, it's not a bad thing to explore the charms of the diminutive.

Fortunately, to make your search for fillers easy, inclinations tend to run in families, so you can use the groups of plants set out in this chapter as guidelines to search further. Certain plant families and groups share characteristics that make them perfectly qualified for the job. So, choose a look and let your imagination roam. Find plants that you can relate to, and put them in a place where they'll fare well. You might be working within a small world, but the possibilities are vast.

BEGONIAS

Some plants were made for Wardian cases. Take begonias, for instance. Begonias bask in high humidity, they delight in indirect light, and they relish close quarters. If ever there was a plant custom-made for terrariums, begonias qualify, hands down. And their cultural preferences are only one facet of the features that make begonias ideal contenders for the position. The diversity of the family also qualifies them for the job. If you happen to be a collector, you can open your wallet plenty and never stray out of the begonia family.

Not only can you exercise your full complement of spending skills, but the begonias you acquire will all look totally different. In the pantheon of plants, begonias are among the most multifaceted members. With leaves ranging from shiny to furry, with spirals, spots, speckles, stripes, and every other foliar marking known to humankind, begonias are addictive, no doubt about it. The differences are sufficiently defined so that even an amateur will recognize that one is

A Brazilian species begonia in flower.

not the same as the next. Furthering the potential of your collecting spree is the fact that many types of begonias don't monopolize much space. Many begonias are sufficiently miniature to fit comfortably in cases throughout their long career.

Rhizomatous begonias

The best begonias for terrariums are in the rhizomatous group. Although that might sound like a limitation, it still gives your creative juices a broad range. Rhizomatous begonias have such diversity, it's difficult to pin a description on them. All send their leaves up from crawling rhizomes, but the foliage has a wide range of shapes, sizes, and colorful markings. Many rhizomatous species are naturally miniature and fond of close, humid quarters. In addition, sprays of small flowers in light pastels often jut up in late winter and spring. Recently, breeders have put an emphasis on downsizing, bulking up the repertoire of compact models with little wonders such as 'Baby Perfection', 'Bethlehem Star', *B. bowerae* 'Nigramarga', 'Brown Twist', 'Enech', 'Fiji Islands', 'Gaystar', 'Nao', *B. prismatocarpa*, 'Royal Lustre', and 'Small Change'.

Rex begonias

Not the easiest plants to host, rex begonias forget their fussy nature and nestle right down into the steady stress-free environment when given a terrarium. Granted, flowers aren't usually in your future with a rex begonia. But instead, these

Rhizomatous and rex begonias in a lantern cloche.

plants boast brightly colored leaves in a broad spectrum of colors, often with bands of several brilliant shades accenting each leaf. Not all rex begonias are sufficiently small to dwell comfortably in a snug terrarium, but there are a handful of dwarf versions available, including 'Dew Drop', 'Shirt Sleeves', 'Vista', and 'Wood Nymph'. However, a word of caution is necessary: If you've got a closed terrarium, ventilation is wise and probably necessary with rex begonias. Rex begonias are susceptible to powdery mildew in constantly stagnant air, a problem that doesn't usually pester the rhizomatous types.

BROMELIADS

You might not think that bromeliads—members of the family that also brings us pineapples—could work in a closed environment. But you have to entertain these unique members of the plant kingdom somewhere. And that somewhere might as well be in a terrarium.

Bromeliads have interesting foliage that's sometimes spiky, often coming in rays from a central point; they're frequently colorful; and they sometimes send up flowering spikes that blossom from equally brilliant bracts after a long drama. Some bromeliads are best grown in a pot in moss. Many (such as the colorful vrieseas) are simply too sizable for easy containment (although if you could find a terrarium of sufficient size, they would be fine). Others are totally epiphytic (growing on trees rather than in the soil). The epiphytic versions—known as air plants—are the simplest to couple with glass. They're easily hung either inside or outside an open-mouthed vase. Best of all, when it comes to low-maintenance plants, bromeliads are the epitome of easy. They're custom-made for the beginner.

Tillandsia—air plant

Often known as air plants, tillandsias have the delightful idiosyncrasy of not needing to be anchored in soil. As their nickname implies, air plants can live happily ever after when suspended in air, and air alone. They're happiest just hanging around—that's how they grow in the wild. And they would be perfectly content being suspended in a glass venue.

These are riveting plants to grow. Many air plants boast fascinating foliage—several are shimmering silver with thick leaves that swirl around. They frequently have felted leaves, and they often form orbs radiating with spiky foliage. Plus, the flowers have festively colored bracts that linger long before and after the actual bright flowers appear (by the way, the spike that produced the flower dies back after its work is done, but it produces pups that carry on the family tradition). Some of the most readily available air plants include *T. caput-medusae, T. concolor, T. fasciculata, T. ionantha,* and *T. nidus.* All are equally easy, and all are conversation pieces.

A glass vase is the perfect solution for juggling air plants and accomplishing their watering needs. Hitch up a wire around the waist (or wherever a piece of wire can get a grip) of

Tillandsia nidus—air plant

whatever air plant you select, bend the wire to make a hook at the end, and voilà! You have a means for hanging your air plant on the lip of a glass vase, either inside or out.

Cryptanthus—earth star

Air plants aren't the only bromeliads to rate as terrarium-worthy. Some cryptanthus, or earth stars, are sufficiently small to qualify for containment. Earth stars have leathery leaves that spring like a star from the base. One of the showiest (and most compact for terrarium purposes) is *Cryptanthus bivittatus* var. *atropurpureus,* forming a 3- to 4-inch-wide star not more than a couple of inches high and offering green and pink wavy leaves. Unlike air plants, earth stars are grounded in terra firma rather than being epiphytic. They should be nestled into mossy soil, but they prefer not to be waterlogged. Because the leaves (although the brittle foliage hardly looks like leaves) are so close to the ground, they can rot from constant contact with extremely damp conditions below.

CARNIVOROUS PLANTS

For anyone who wants to invite a little cloak and dagger into their home, carnivorous plants can be willing accomplices. Not all carnivorous plants belong to the same family. But because these plants all share the decidedly weird quirk of ingesting meat as part of their diet, they're grouped together.

No, these plants don't bite. At least, they won't take a chunk out of your children; but they're death to mosquitoes. Most carnivorous plants consume insects. By definition, they attract prey, capture it, kill it, digest it, and assimilate the prey's nutrients into their system. If that sounds slightly yucky to you, maybe these plants and you aren't a great match. But if your curiosity is piqued, then you might want to consider adopting a Venus flytrap, pitcher plant, sundew, or something else in the plant kingdom that isn't a vegetarian. For those who thrill at the prospect of watching flies getting snagged and consumed, this is your type of show. And a glass bowl offers a ringside view as well as appropriate accommodations to house your little resident carnivore. However, if you find the concept intriguing but aren't sure whether you need to watch continual demonstrations, a closed cloche that doesn't permit insects to enter might be just the thing.

Dionaea muscipula—Venus flytrap

That notorious little housefly eliminator, the Venus flytrap is sufficiently mainstream to be found at supermarkets. Jutting from a rhizome below ground, a Venus flytrap's leaves bear an uncanny resemblance to gaping jaws complete with pointed fangs, plus glands that secrete the sort of mucilage a fly might find attractive. Before dinner, those jaws lay ajar to expose tiny hairs. If a hapless fly happens to land on the open pad, it disturbs the hairs, which rapidly (very rapidly) trigger the trap to shut. The fangs prevent the meal from escaping, and its bodily fluids are slowly digested to feed the flytrap. Afterward, that arm of the plant is sacrificed—it rots with the carcass of the consumed bug.

A lesser-known bromeliad *Neoregelia marmorata.*

Venus flytraps can be grown only in a terrarium environment indoors; no matter how moist your in-house climate happens to be, it probably won't be sufficiently wet for this bog plant. In a terrarium, this meat eater can remain happy for quite a while. Many carnivores are fond of bright light, which can be a problem in a closed case—an open-mouthed container might be a happier hunting ground. And a happy Venus flytrap is a hungry Venus flytrap. Often the trigger action doesn't work unless this carnivore is content.

Drosera capensis—sundew

With tiny, spoon-shaped leaves radiating from a central base, sundews have tentacles covered with glands that secrete a substance sufficiently sweet and sticky to lure and then capture a meal. In sunbeams, those tentacles sparkle like jewels. Apparently, bugs are lured toward the treasure. Once a sundew has dinner in close proximity, its tentacles roll in a deadly embrace. And from there, it takes about fifteen minutes for the struggle to be won. Eventually, the insect dies of exhaustion or asphyxiation. Sundews are small enough to fit easily into an apothecary jar or Mason jar. Open the lid if you want to watch them dine.

Sarracenia spp.—pitcher plant

Exquisitely veined, hooded funnels are used to do the sarracenias'—or pitcher plants'—dirty deeds. Nectarlike secretions on the lip of the funnel attract the plant's dinner, and the inside of the

Sarracenia sp.—pitcher plant

funnel is slippery. In the case of Sarracenia purpurea, one of the more readily available pitcher plants, rainwater collects inside that slippery funnel for the express purpose of drowning whatever is clueless enough to crawl in (in a pinch, and where rainwater isn't likely to happen, you could use a watering can to fill up the pitchers). Here again, this bog plant prefers bright light, so an open-mouthed terrarium is not only the ideal living environment but an effective meal ticket as well.

All pitcher plants thrive in terrariums. Some may even send up flowers, if they're particularly happy (and well fed). The flowers are large, nodding, and look somewhat like parachutes. Their tall stems also make a lidless terrarium the most practical venue.

FERNS

Ferns were there in the beginning. The prototype for the terrarium trend caught fire when Nathaniel Ward had the burning desire to bring ferns into his city apartment and was continually frustrated by their failure to thrive in that environment until they were sequestered in glass. The fact that he never forgot that initial attraction says a lot about the seduction of fronds.

The world of ferns is vast. Back in Nathaniel Ward's day, he had access only to the hardy ferns found in the forests of the countryside. And yet, he was smitten. Now (thanks to Ward's cases and their role in bringing the tropics to us) we have at our beck and call such an array of ferny architectural forms that you can literally achieve any look you favor, from frilly to sleek. The diversity is uncanny. With a world of various fronds, crosiers, and fiddleheads at your command, you could easily furnish your home in the lush green of ferns and never, ever grow bored.

Denizens of the understory of the forest and rain forest, ferns don't want or need bright light, a trait that makes terrariums and ferns simpatico. Most homes have places where light levels are low, especially in centrally located gathering rooms, and ferns perform remarkably in just those conditions. The light coming in through your windows, no matter what direction they face, is probably sufficient to satisfy a fern. Instead of struggling with flowering plants that are continually frustrated in their need for sun, you can easily fulfill ferns' needs.

ABOVE Only in summer, when a radiator is not in use, can it cradle a Nephrolepis under a cloche. **OPPOSITE** *Hemionitis arifolia*, the heart fern, stands in the company of cut dahlias and zinnias.

All ferns are grateful to be coupled with glass; the following list is just a small sampling of the ferns that you can combine with a closed case. They dote on the high humidity that a terrarium provides.

Adiantum spp.—maidenhair ferns

Some ferns demand a terrarium. Maidenhairs are a good example. Maidenhair ferns typically have a black, shiny central rib (known as the rachis) running up their fronds with tiny, pale green, fan-shaped leaves (known as segments) attached. The hybrids have names such as 'Sea Foam', which gives you an idea of what the presentation looks like. They generally stand about 6 to 9 inches tall, although there are smaller versions.

Maidenhairs are custom-made for terrariums sizewise, and their temperament also makes them well suited to terrarium life. Maidenhairs have a tendency to go dormant indoors, especially during winter, unless they're given the benefit of a toasty glass case. The stable environment takes the edge off the climate that isn't mother's milk for a maidenhair. And while they're basking in their ideal growing conditions, they capture the essence of the forest floor within the glass enclosure.

Davallia, Humata, and Polypodium— footed ferns

Not everyone finds the footed ferns amusing. Some folks get the willies when they encounter the groping mass of appendages typical of this group. If a confused mass of furry little rhizomes

reminds you of tarantulas, these ferns might not be for you. But if you think of them as resembling a squirrel's feet, you might be on firmer ground. And really, when a footed fern is well grown (a terrarium helps in this endeavor), the foliage covers the feet. There's the squirrel's foot fern (*D. mariesii*), the rabbit's foot fern (*D. fejeensis* 'Plumosa'), the bear's foot fern (*Humata tyermannii*), and the green serpent (*Polypodium formosanum*). All have silver fur covering rhizomes roughly the width of your pinkie, except the green serpent. It has lime green feet that bear an uncanny resemblance to a mass of green worms.

Dryopteris filix-mas—male fern

No wonder Nathaniel Ward was delighted when he could at last entertain a male fern in his parlor due to his bottle with a stopper. Although the male fern is prevalent in the wild, it's still a treat indoors. Adorned with frothy, lacy, deeply segmented, pale green leaves, the male fern and its many sports (also occasionally found in the wild) often have all sorts of frilly crests and segments to the foliage. Although they eventually become large, they usually remain under 2 feet in size, and their energy is somewhat crimped in a terrarium, so they generally stay within bounds. As you might suspect, there's a counterpart to the male fern—the lady fern, *Athyrium filix-femina*. It has even more diversity in frond frilliness available in its sports and is equally suitable for a terrarium.

Hemionitis arifolia—heart fern

Not all ferns look like they belong in the family. For example, the fronds of the heart fern bear no resemblance to your typical fern foliage. As you can gather from the nickname, they're heart-shaped—held on wiry stipes just a few inches above the ground. The heart fern can be found at garden centers. But without a terrarium, it won't thrive for long in the average home. A humid terrarium keeps the heart-shaped fronds from curling and drying out. It's the tool that allows you to enjoy a decidedly different tropical fern—native to Sri Lanka, India, Myanmar, Taiwan, and thereabouts—that would not normally be within your realm.

Pellaea rotundifolia—button fern

Some plants demand a terrarium in order to survive indoors, and the button fern is in that camp. As the name implies, the low-growing black midrib is lined with a row of round, mahogany-colored leaves, rendering this fern unique and highly desirable. Although it's difficult to grow, the button fern isn't hard to find—it's often offered at garden centers. Unfortunately, the moment you bring one home from a greenhouse, it begins its decline—unless you can plunk the plant into a terrarium. For a button fern, a closed terrarium is preferable.

GESNERIADS

Gesneriads are members of the African violet family. And when you begin to explore the clan, you'll find there's plenty of collection-worthy fodder that respond well to terrariums. Members of this group like and need high humidity. Not only that, but they strongly dislike fluctuations in temperature. They prefer evenly warm growing conditions without a sharp drop in temperature at night. They don't mind moisture, but they dislike water on the leaves. Most critically, they detest direct sun and their leaves will burn if subjected to bright sunbeams. All of these traits work in your favor when growing in glass. Just make sure not to allow any sun to fall on your terrarium. Sometimes that's a challenge. Pull the terrarium away from the window, and you're probably safe.

One word of caution: Most members of this group don't like to sit in water. So it might be to everyone's best advantage to plant your member of the African violet family in a container to tuck in glass rather than directly in a terrarium. And a ventilated case might be better than a closed cloche.

The big perk of the gesneriad group is the flowers. Not many terrarium plants are vigorous bloomers, but many gesneriads are incredibly enthusiastic producers of flowers. For other members of the plant kingdom, blossoms are a factor that comes with brighter light than a terrarium can tolerate. Gesneriads are a delightful exception; most of the terrarium types blossom energetically throughout the year in indirect sun.

Codonanthes

Although many members of the gesneriad family have loose, wandering branches, the codonanthes remain more compact than most of their hanging relatives, usually remaining below 6 inches in height. Not only do codonanthes have tidy, tiny, shining leaves on their lax stems, they also produce quaint, tubular blossoms. 'Aurora' is one of the best bloomers, producing a crop of yellowish pink flowers. Each flower is less than an inch long, but their discrete dimensions are perfectly suited to a terrarium—where they enjoy conditions that are a gesneriad's dream.

Episcia and *Alsobia*—flame violets

When you want flowers, and you want them striking and bright, then you can't do better than flame violets (*Episcia* spp.) for a terrarium. Flame violets pack a double punch, offering handsome leaves as well as colorful flowers. The creeping

Streptocarpus—Cape primrose

foliage has a range that compares favorably with that of begonias: cultivars are available in plain green (often with silver netting overlaying the foliage) as well as shades of copper and brown, or with pink and cream markings. Add flowers that are the size of a quarter, come in profusion, and are various shades of pink and red, and you have a winning combination. If this all sounds like too much of a wallop, go for the closely related *Alsobia dianthiflora* instead. It's got roaming, small, solid green leaves enhanced by white flowers.

Saintpaulia—African violet

The genuine African violets, the best-known members of the gesneriad group, are actually cultivars of *Saintpaulia velutina*, native to Tanzania. So they do hail from Africa, but they bear no relation to true violets whatsoever. Their foliage is similar to that of violas, however, hence the nickname. They form tidy rosettes of furry foliage like a little nosegay (dark green was originally the standard, but now they come with variegated cream and pink leaves), with sprays of blossoms sprouting from the center. Those flowers come in an astonishingly varied color range, including all manner of blues from periwinkle to navy, pinks, reds, and whites. Initially, the single flowers resembled violet blooms. Nowadays the double-petaled versions are more popular, and they mimic miniature rosebuds. Plus, the beauty of an African violet is that it's nearly always blossoming. But be warned: Patrolling for past blossoms before they brown and court mold can be a full-time job.

Saintpaulia—African violet

Sinningia pusilla

When you've got a plant that is such a micro-midget that it can be easily grown in a thimble, a terrarium seems like the best venue to profile its charms. *Sinningia pusilla* cultivars have leaves about the size of the nail on your little finger growing in a tiny rosette. And yet the frequent blossoms are vigorous and held in tiny clusters above the leaves. They are the epitome of quaint. These relatives of gloxinias (that would be *S. speciosa*—a species whose hybrids are generally too large for the average terrarium) also share the trait of occasionally going dormant. Don't throw out the wee thing if it slips into slumber—just wait for the leaves to reemerge.

Streptocarpus cvs.—Cape primrose

Cape primroses are not related to actual primulas, although their leaves are similar. Long, slender, heavily veined, and like plush velvet, Cape primrose foliage grows in rosette form—like that of a primrose. From the center of that rosette comes a nearly continuous supply of blossoms held on rigid stems. The tubular flowers usually begin at an inch in diameter, with hybrids that are slightly larger. And the color range includes all shades of blue, purple, pink, red, and white, with bicolors also being part of the brew. But the characteristic that renders Cape primroses infinitely compatible for terrariums is their temperature requirements. They pout and refuse to blossom when the thermometer slips below 65°F at night. A terrarium is the best way to keep them snug and protected, especially for those of us who turn the thermostat down at night.

MOSSES

All mosses respond favorably to being grown within glass. Actually, an enclosure of some sort is the only way to go. Mosses are high maintenance without a glass facilitator. Even the hardy outdoor mosses that sulk immediately when brought indoors will rally when given the benefit of a moist, closed environment. Rather than trying to mist a hardy moss 24/7 to quench its need for moisture, enclose it in glass, sit back, and watch it go emerald. (It's been said that you would have to mist every fifteen minutes around the clock to really effectively raise the relative humidity in a home atmosphere.)

Moss should not be collected from the wild. You should never go out into the woods and come home with the souvenir of a moss tussock. Although mosses might not be endangered (yet), they have the potential of disappearing. Some pioneer mosses make good headway, but many rarer secondary mosses are painfully slow growing, requiring years to make a clump the size of a baseball. You don't want to disturb something that fragile. So leave it be. Instead, purchase moss from a moss farm where it has been nursery grown and propagated.

That's the hardy mosses. Much easier to obtain are the tropical mosses—selaginellas, occasionally called club mosses or spike mosses. The club mosses that you generally find at garden centers and nurseries are tender and will not withstand freezing winter temperatures. Indoors, however, they do just fine—especially if given the protection of a terrarium. Perhaps a little puffier and looser than the tight little buns made by the crawling mosses found in our woods, selaginellas otherwise look quite similar.

All mosses love high humidity. Not only do they respond to closed cases, they dote on tight confinement. Mosses are custom-made for a bell jar with a lid, a clear cookie jar tightly shut, or a tightly glazed Wardian case. In fact, they are so grateful for the enclosure that they can be aggressive companions for less rambunctious plants such as begonias. Solitary confinement isn't a bad way to go. Or use ferns as allies. Another great pairing is to plant a terrarium with moss along with spring bulbs that will go dormant. It's a creative means of keeping the terrarium rolling when the bulbs are history.

Mosses are low-maintenance, but they do need to be divided. At the very least, they should receive occasional haircuts to reduce the density of their tangled mass. Reaching in and scooping out a bit of moss—reducing it by half at regular intervals, depending on how fast your moss is expanding—is a wise moss "farming" practice. The moss will thrive because of it.

Selaginella kraussiana and *S. k.* 'Aurea'— spreading club mosses

The most commonly found mosses for growing indoors are the spreading club mosses, *Selaginella kraussiana* and its golden twin *S. k.* 'Aurea'. They look identical to each other, except for their slight color variation. They are nonhardy kin in a genus that has many members that will tolerate freezing temperatures in winter. Together, they can make a wonderful interweave, although both

Selaginella kraussiana 'Aurea'—spreading club moss

Selaginella uncinata—peacock moss

Selaginella umbrosa—red club moss

are sufficiently energetic ultimately to get into each other's hair. Spreading club mosses will form a little, tightly woven mound of shimmering color with uneven tufts of foliage stretching out in tiers—like a tiny evergreen chamaecyparis hedge. And they expand by creeping along, sending down roots for anchors as they roam. In a humid environment, the roots might be visible above the soil level—which is no cause for concern; but if you find it disconcerting, scoop up the clump and bury the aboveground roots. *S. k.* 'Frosty Fern' is readily available, especially around the winter holidays; it has silver edging accenting the tips of its foliage. Most club mosses wander, but certain versions are more apt to form little round tussocks that are easy to keep within bounds; *S. k.* 'Brownii' is a good example of a moss with manners. It expands slowly and doesn't roam, but then, it's not so readily divided and shared as are the common club mosses.

S. uncinata—peacock moss

Another similar species is *S. uncinata,* the peacock or rainbow moss. Like a peacock, the branchlets sparkle with color and appear purple or blue. This is an energetic traveler, covering ground. Divide this moss to keep it in bounds.

ORCHIDS

Although they're divinely beautiful, and although they make your heart go pitter-patter and your nostrils quiver with their phenomenally intense fragrances, orchids aren't within everybody's reach. Out there naked in the average room, many orchids wouldn't fare particularly well. Fascinating to behold, orchids might be everything you would want in a plant that's flourishing in your home, but orchid envy is all that's possible for most people.

Enlist the help of a terrarium, and growing orchids can become your expertise. You can secure those sensational blossoms and display them in a setting befitting their grandeur, and you can do it in any room that's got an east- or west-facing window.

Almost any orchid will thrive in a terrarium. And the diversity of this group of plants is just awesome. You can have a very expensive field day. With a terraruim, there's a way to give that big, beautiful, pricey plant the play it deserves.

Orchids perform with gusto when they're given the additional humidity that terrariums furnish. A terrarium also eases a watering regime that some gardeners find daunting—most orchids are grown in moss or bark, and the water runs straight through. Normally, drinks are served every few days. In a terrarium, the schedule is much more lax.

Ludisia discolor—jewel orchid

Although the jewel orchid readily makes blossoms when it's happy, the leaves are the big thrill here.

The foliage is about 2 to 3 inches long, buff black, and etched with pink veins. It's quite a show, especially when the new growth unfurls with its burgundy leaf backs. Generally remaining under a foot in height, a jewel orchid needs a terrarium not only for the moisture but also because it prefers nighttime temperatures between 65° and 75°F. When it has the type of environment it craves, the jewel orchid sends up spires of fragrant white blossoms with yellow markings. In a terrarium, give a jewel orchid a bed of moss to sink its roots into.

Paphiopedilum spp. and cvs.—tropical lady's slippers

Whimsy can be had on the windowsill, especially if you grow tropical lady's slippers. These easily grown performers are the clowns of the orchid clan, bearing pert, slightly comical, elflike blossoms (if you see the lower lip as a big, broad grin and the upper petals as a cap) and long, ground-hugging leaves. Some of the tropical lady's slipper orchids (especially *Paphiopedilum* Maudiae types) boast handsomely mottled leaves that stage a show without the need of flowers (although flowers will probably be part of the picture, eventually, with the help of your terrarium). The blossom show can occur more than once a year. Not only that but, enclosed in glass, the flowers can linger for weeks; four to six weeks isn't uncommon. And during that performance run, you won't be worrying continually about watering, humidity levels, and generally playing the good host because your terrarium will be taking care of all those chores.

Phalaenopsis spp.—moth orchids

If you're new to orchids, moth orchids are a great place to begin. First of all, they're fulfilling—although the thick, broad leaves aren't particularly exciting, the flower spikes hold many flowers that look like a horde of moths or butterflies taking flight. The show continues over several weeks, sometimes a few months. In addition, moth orchids are so easy to entertain that they don't really need a terrarium to perform. In fact, the flower spike is often too tall to fit in confinement. Fortunately, there are dwarf moth orchids now available, and they are the perfect size for a terrarium.

ORNAMENTAL GRASSES

Although diminutive is the obvious way to go when thinking terrariums, glass vases and jars can also cradle larger plants to render your indoors a green-friendly space. Take grasses, for example. Everyone is familiar with grass; it's a universal point of reference. Of course, no one is going to plant a lawn in a terrarium. But it's amazing what you *can* grow in a container. Sow seeds of cat grass (generally packaged with wheat seeds), watch it sprout and shoot up, and you will secure instant summer no matter what time of year happens to be transpiring outdoors. All sorts of ornamental grasses can cohabitate indoors. And many enjoy (or at least endure) the glass treatment. Grasses don't need glass, but it's one way to accommodate them indoors and bring their texture and sleek silhouette into your life.

Because they don't really want or need high humidity, most grasses shouldn't be housed in a closed case. In fact, many become too tall for that sort of confined treatment anyway. The exception would be the tufted sedges, which are the small-fry of grasses. For the vast majority of grasslike plants, you'll need to enlist a vase or glass jar large enough to balance the bulk of foliage that springs up from the base and the wad of roots that comes along with the gig. Of course, it's necessary to select a grass that remains within bounds. The larger ornamental giants of the garden, with their stately plumes of flowers, massive colonies of blades, and potentially glass-busting root systems, are never going to work in a confined space. But find a tall, slender *Pennisetum setaceum*, for example, and you've discovered a plant that prefers moisture at its roots, tolerates a fairly humid environment, and can be contained over the short haul.

ABOVE *Isolepis cernua*—fiber-optic grass
OPPOSITE *Paphiopedilum*—tropical lady's slipper orchid

Acorus gramineus 'Pusillus'—sedge

If you want to host one of the tiniest ornamental plants around, go for this tiny plant, occasionally sold as *Acorus minima*, especially if you're composing a scene and want to use something reminiscent of an iris, scaled down drastically—it basically looks like a minute tuft. Slightly larger and also available with striking variegation would be other *A. gramineus* cultivars.

Cyperus spp.—papyrus

Grow a papyrus in a deep glass jar, and not only have you found a solution to standing its tall blades upright without staking, but you've also saved yourself from continually lugging water. These are striking plants with a round topknot of spiky foliage and flowers crowning a tall grasslike spike. Semiaquatic, the papyruses are such heavy drinkers that you'll still have to fetch water for them now and then, but the duties are diminished considerably. Eventually, the roots will outgrow the container and it will be necessary to divide the plant.

Isolepis cernua—fiber-optic grass

Fiber-optic grass is a sterling example of a suitable specimen for terrariums. It's readily available as a houseplant. And it's a fascinating little plant, brandishing a series of tiny little tufts at the tips of each blade. Of the proper dimensions for indoors, fiber-optic grass stands less than a foot in height and doesn't make an expansive clump. The only problem is, it's aquatic—making this fiber-optic phenomenon difficult to host indoors unless you're constant with the watering can. But give it a glass enclosure, and presto! It becomes a low-maintenance plant.

PEPEROMIAS

Peperomias are like foundation plantings for terrariums. They're predictable but dependable, and almost essential. You can hang your hat on a peperomia. Rock-solid simple to grow, absolutely unfazed by any sort of growing conditions, peperomias will soldier on courageously without a terrarium. Members of the same family that brings us pepper (the kind you grind for seasoning), they wouldn't bat an eyelash if you forgot to water or neglected to feed them. They didn't earn the nickname "radiator plants" for nothing. Cool with being stashed just about anywhere, they never pout. But bare naked without some help from glass, they won't shine either.

It's highly likely that peperomias are waiting patiently for you at a nearby garden center. In fact, they'll be hanging around pretty much anywhere plants are sold—even supermarkets. And most peperomias have the proper dimensions and demeanor to be elevated to life in a terrarium.

Cyperus alternifolius, umbrella plant, and *Juncus effusus*, common rush, can grow on a radiator when the heating system isn't in use.

As for guises, there are many. Although there aren't as many peperomias in cultivation as, say, begonias, the group has similar diversity. The only trait that all the members of this family have in common is the world's most boring blossoms. In truth, the flowers on a peperomia bear an unfortunate resemblance to rat tails. If you like that sort of thing, let the blooms stay. If not, simply remove the long, slender whip. And what will remain is fairly good-looking foliage. Some peperomias are upright, some are silver with a grainy surface, several make little rosettes from the base like violets or primroses and produce round leaves like those of water lilies, some resemble succulents. But none need bright light—rendering them custom-suited for terrariums.

Peperomia caperata—emerald ripple

One of the most common peperomias, emerald ripple, comes in many variations on the same theme. The foliage has long leaf stems and is deeply textured, puckered, and round. All the versions slowly make small clumps and grow no larger than 6 inches or so, making them ideal for a terrarium. There are many different leaf shades available beyond the plain green—versions with silver, burgundy, and cream-edged foliage are all within easy reach.

P. glabella—cyperus peperomia

Found growing wild in Florida, native to South and Central America as well as the West Indies, the cyperus peperomia is an absolutely fail-safe plant for a beginner. Roaming around on lax but also succulent stems, the thick and shiny elliptic-shaped leaves are green with a rose flush. The beauty of this plant is not only that it's unkillable, it's also a cinch to propagate. Just tuck a runner into a moss-filled pot and pop it into a terrarium.

P. incana—felted peperomia

The peperomia genus is incredibly large, with more than 1,000 members and similarly impressive diversity. Unlike most of its kin, the felted peperomia has 2- to 3-inch broad, thick, silver matte leaves on upright stems. Slow growing, it won't make sufficient headway to require continual graduation from terrarium to larger terrarium. Often topped by equally silver rat-tail flowers, it's one of the more exciting peperomias around.

LEFT A cutting of *Peperomia glabella*. OPPOSITE A mini greenhouse holds (from left to right) *Peperomia asperula*, *P. rubella*, and *P. rotundifolia* var. *pilosior*.

P. peruviana—miniature watermelon peperomia

With a similar growth habit and form to the emerald ripple, the miniature watermelon peperomia has small round leaves on the tips of long leaf stems. In the case of the miniature watermelon peperomia, each shiny leaf isn't much larger than your thumbnail, with markings similar to those on a watermelon rind. A vigorous bloomer, you'll get plenty of rat tails on this one. It's virtually indestructible in a terrarium or on the windowsill.

P. rotundifolia var. *pilosior*—prostrate peperomia

Just to cover all the bases as far as growth habits are concerned, there's the prostrate peperomia. Its array of tiny, creeping, round leaves lie flat against the soil. Each leaf has a complex silver pattern, making this one of the most intriguing ground covers for a small scene in a terrarium. And it grows rapidly—a trait that's also ideal for the contained life.

PILEAS

Often mentioned in the same breath as peperomias, pileas are similar to that group as far as foliage is concerned. They have brittle leaves on spiky stems, and they're sedately intriguing. However, pileas belong to a totally different family than peperomias: they're related to nettles. The flowers bear evidence of the family connection. The flowers are like a fluffy nest of squiggly filaments tucked close to the foliage. Often those filaments are blush pink or maroon. Sometimes, however, you have to look carefully for the flowers—they're definitely not showstoppers, and they tend to blend in.

Pileas are pretty much inseparable from peperomias from a cultivation standpoint. Like beefed-up versions of peperomias, some will become too large for a terrarium with time—the Persian shield, also known as the aluminum plant (*Pilea cadierei*), could grow in a terrarium, and would be a nice adornment with its shiny, metallic silver leaves, but it would need the ample space of a large hurricane lamp or big Wardian case in order to thrive. However, the smaller members of this genus are custom-made for a terrarium.

Pilea glauca 'Aquamarine'

A loose ground cover, *Pilea glauca* 'Aquamarine' makes a dense tangle of thin, trailing, deep burgundy stems sparingly clad in the tiniest silver (with a bluish cast) leaves. It's adorable to behold but be prepared with your clippers to prune off overly enthusiastic growth on this roaming pilea. Besides that, it's extremely easy, lending a welcome dash of bright color to the venue.

Pilea nummularifolia—creeping Charlie

P. involucrata—friendship plant

I'm guessing that the friendship plant was given its common name because it's one of those legendary "pass-along plants" that went from gardener to gardener, cuttings slipped into glasses of water and then potted to become houseplants. The friendship plant is as handsome as it is low-maintenance, offering tiers of rounded, green-and-silver-striped leaves always showing a hint of their blush pink undersides. Densely stacked, the pink stems can be glimpsed between the leaves. And flowers are also an occasional perk. Nothing could be easier than the friendship plant—it can grow in or out of a terrarium. However, its oddball progeny *P. i.* 'Moon Valley', occasionally known as the cat's tongue plant for its prickly-textured leaves, is a whole different story as far as cultivation is

concerned. In a normal house, it will pout unless given a home in a terrarium.

P. microphylla—artillery plant

Some plants should only be grown in a confined space, and the artillery plant is a case in point. Consider some of its other common names—the gunpowder plant, the pistol plant—and you've got some inkling of this pilea's propagating energy. Growing with a mass of pinhead-size, pale green leaves like a froth of sea foam, the nondescript flowers are almost too small to be seen with the naked eye. Nevertheless, they disperse seeds everywhere. They're detested as a virulent weed by greenhouse growers, especially in Florida, where greenhouses are rife. And they escape into gardens as well. Grown in a closed terrarium, they are contained and not so apt to become a nuisance.

P. nummularifolia—creeping Charlie

Maybe creeping Charlie isn't the most wildly exciting plant on the planet. But it certainly is easy to grow. It has apple green, thick, rounded leaves closely and densely held on trailing stems. Those leaves have an intriguing texture, like the pile on a carpet. And the plants are very easily propagated. Without a terrarium, however, you would probably never notice creeping Charlie. Climbing out of an open-mouthed terrarium, it makes a nice presentation.

OTHER OPTIONS

Many plants just happen to have all the right characteristics to make them well suited to life in containment. Although they don't belong in the families and groups that we think of when we think terrariums, lots of plants have what it takes to be terrarium-worthy. Most are small, and some are just low-light-loving, amiable types that thrive where the going is tight, warm, and humid.

The following pages describe a handful of the many possibilities for filling terrariums. But, beyond these suggestions, don't hesitate to launch your own experiments. When in doubt, give a promising plant a try and monitor the situation. What can you lose? And you have everything to gain.

Ajuga reptans—bugleweed

Because it grows perfectly well in shade, bugleweed can be contained in a terrarium. This popular frost-hardy garden ground cover thrives in the most hellish locations imaginable. It is frighteningly easy to cultivate and can grow practically anywhere—including your living room. And also on the plus side, bugleweeds are inexpensive, readily available, they might even be found in a backyard near you. In which case, go ahead and dig a clump—there's usually plenty on hand (of course, ask first, if the garden isn't your own). The only problem is that most bugleweeds are too fast moving for a terrarium. Fortunately, there are tiny versions that will thrive, such as 'Chocolate Chip' and 'Metallica Crispa Purpurea'—both with handsome bronze foliage. And 'Burgundy Glow', with red, cream, and green mottled leaves, is not as speedy as most bugleweeds. In addition, a bugleweed might even send up the further entertainment of little blue blossoms on short spires in spring.

Biophytum sensitivum—sensitive plant

Not only is the sensitive plant a wonderful tiny palm tree look-alike perfect for anyone who wants to vicariously enjoy Florida in the middle of the winter, but it also has another gimmick. As the common name implies, sensitive plants fold their leaves at night and when you touch the foliage. So you've got a naked little stem with a cluster of palm-tree-type leaves perched on top, and those leaves have movement. As a further bonus, sensitive plants produce a continual supply of tiny pink flowers that result in a plentiful crop of seedpods. And that's a good thing for a plant with a short life. Because eventually, your little faux palm begins to lose oomph and drop leaves and will need replacing with a younger version. You can have the next crop waiting in the wings, grown from the seed you've planted.

Cuphea hyssopifolia—Hawaiian heather, elfin herb

Under low-light conditions, not everything will flower. The Hawaiian heather, however, blossoms nonstop throughout the seasons despite diminished light. The flowers aren't large, but they're profuse and dapple the entire plant. Plus, Hawaiian heather is incredibly easy to grow. Forming a very compact little bush (it can be pruned to 6 inches or less), this cuphea looks for all the world like a tiny shrub—the ideal actor to play the part of a scaled-down tree in a mini landscape. Due to the fact that they're fond of being pruned, it's not difficult to keep Hawaiian heathers within bounds.

Other plants that might love a terrarium include (from left to right) *Ficus pumila* 'Snowflake', *Ajuga reptans* 'Burgundy Glow', and *Hoya lacunosa*.

Cyanotis kewensis—teddy bear vine

Related to the easy-to-grow tradescantia, the teddy bear vine has tiny, long, slender leaves covered with plush brown fur. The leaves trail happily over the ground with zest. In fact, keeping abreast of this energetic plant can prove difficult. But, given room to roam, the teddy bear vine is the sort of plant that anyone can learn to love. And if it begins to encroach on its neighbors, just divide it up to share with friends of all ages.

ABOVE *Ficus pumila* cultivar—creeping fig
OPPOSITE *Cuphea hyssopifolia*—Hawaiian heather

Ficus pumila cvs.—creeping fig

Although the typical creeping fig is much too athletic a creepy-crawler to play well in close proximity with others, there are smaller versions that mind their manners. Looking nothing like the figs that Adam and Eve accessed in their moment of shame, these petite family members have leaves no larger than a dime. Not only that, but they crawl along, spilling over the sides of whatever they're growing in, forming a lacework of leaves. And leaves are the complete show here—these figs don't form fruit. There is a variegated version with white-edged foliage ('Snowflake'). There's an oak-leaved version ('Quercifolia') and an especially tiny carpet type ('Minima'). All are energetic and might need to be pruned back. That's easy enough, just snip away.

And speaking of figs, there's a tiny version of the ever-popular old standby *Ficus benjamina* called 'Too Little' and it's perfect for terrariums. A lilliputian rendition of a tree with woody stems and teardrop-shaped, slightly curly leaves, it can be used as a mini tree in a scene. Plus, it's just as easy as its big brother—the office-building cliché—to cultivate.

Fittonia verschaffeltii—mosaic plant

Forming a neat little cluster of intriguing leaves, the mosaic plant isn't much of a bloomer, but there's ample intrigue with the leaves alone. Always tidy and definitely slow-paced, the foliage has electric lipstick pink veins running like a network of nerves against forest green leaves, forming a fascinating picture. Set off in glass, the mosaic plant is particularly noteworthy. There's a white-veined version as well (*Fittonia verschaffeltii* var. *argyroneura*). Both are great for the beginner.

Hedera helix—ivy

Few plants are easier to grow than an ivy. From the ivy climbing on college walls to the ground cover around suburban houses, ivy is something that most people associate with the outdoors. Why not bring it into your life on a closer basis?

Plus, ivy is a plant that everyone can grow. You certainly don't need a terrarium for this one; it could be happy just about anywhere, north-facing windowsills included. But then you'd have to water it regularly. A terrarium will shoulder that task.

Any ivy will grow happily in a terrarium. But most standard-size ivies fill in with too much haste and thoroughness. The standard versions aren't polite companions for other terrarium plants, and you won't be able to love them, leave

ABOVE *Fittonia verschaffeltii*—mosaic plant
OPPOSITE *Hedera helix* 'My Heart'—ivy

Clockwise from top left: *Pilea* 'Aquamarine', *Ficus pumila* cultivar, *Soleirolia soleirolii*, and *Sagina subulata*

version is *M. axillaris,* which forms a little bun of wiry stems. It can coexist blissfully with other plants. Both produce flowers that are best seen with a magnifier. Fruit follows, and it's not a whole lot larger than the blossoms.

Saxifraga stolonifera—strawberry geranium

Here's another instance when a common name can confuse identity. This plant isn't a strawberry or a geranium. But it creeps around just like a strawberry or a geranium (another nickname— mother of thousands—tells all), with runners that lay down roots and form plantlets where they roam. Plus, the strawberry geranium has beautifully mottled, plush velvety green, rounded leaves. Best of all, this particular saxifraga likes high humidity. It's actually hardy to USDA Zone 5, so it might remind you of the garden—especially if your experience is with shady gardens. Although the plain vanilla *Saxifraga stolonifera* is not difficult to grow, 'Tricolor' (alias 'Magic Carpet') is a killer to cultivate, in a terrarium or otherwise.

Serissa foetida—snow rose

If tiny plants that impersonate larger players in the garden tickle your fancy, or if you're trying to create a mini garden scene under glass, then the snow rose is essential. Serissas form tiny bushes with minute leaves. Plus, they produce little blossoms in quantity. They really do look like a miniature version of the rose.

For them to grow best, remain compact, and blossom, you'll need to give snow roses as much light as a closed case will tolerate without burning. Snow roses come with white or pink flowers, in double ('Flore Pleno') or single form. Several have variegated leaves, and the smallest version is 'Kyoto'—which forms a tight network of branches but rarely blossoms.

Soleirolia soleirolii—baby's tears

The froth of tiny leaves on baby's tears is absolutely adorable. Each leaf isn't a whole lot larger than a pinhead, and thousands of them scamper around when this ground cover is happy. The problem is, although everyone loves this cutie, very few people can grow it, and that's where a terrarium comes in.

A terrarium is pretty much a necessity if you're going to host baby's tears. And a closed case is preferable. However, be warned— happy baby's tears will run rampant. It's not always a great bedfellow, unless you're letting it scamper below plants meant to look like shrubs or trees.

Solenostemon 'India Frills'—coleus

Solenostemon scutellaroides—coleus

Everybody calls these plants coleus, even if scientists have changed the name to solenostemon. You've undoubtedly encountered coleus outdoors. You might even indulge in a few coleus in your own gardens or patio containers. Well, here's an opening for coleus to come indoors and continue their antics when summer has come and gone. Made for the shade, easily grown, and requiring only a smattering of attention with pruning shears to keep the plant in good shape, coleus is perfectly contented with containment. Needless to say, you'd be wise to adopt one of the smaller varieties such as 'Inky Fingers', 'India Frills', or 'Charlie McCarthy'—because some coleus can be a handful sizewise. If you have a larger version, use a terrarium to start cuttings for next year's garden, and keep them confined until they flex their muscles, requiring larger quarters.

Tetranema roseum—Mexican foxglove

One of the most entertaining elements of terrariums is searching out miniature plants that impersonate familiar players in the garden. And that's where the Mexican foxglove comes in handy. It has long, tubular blossoms—just like foxglove, although greatly scaled down. From a tidy rosette of dark green leaves, little nosegays of purple flowers pop. No need to wait for the show, since the plant is almost always flowering. And flowers are a plus in a shaded terrarium. Beyond the nonstop production of flowers, Mexican foxglove doesn't really do much growthwise, which is optimal, because you don't want fast-moving plants in a terrarium. Keep Mexican foxglove in a moist situation—it wilts easily.

Tolmiea menziesii—piggyback plant

In a world that's fond of gimmicks, the piggyback plant gives you something to watch. Each velvety, maple-shaped leaf has a tiny plantlet growing from the center. Sometimes the tiny plantlet balances yet another tinier plantlet on top. It's just adorable, and it's an instant

Plants That Won't Grow in Terrariums

PLANTS THAT thrive in a terrarium are an elite set. Although the parameters are probably much broader than you imagine, the traits that make a plant appropriate for a terrarium are fairly circumscribed. Not just anything is going to love life in a glass enclosure; not all plants will thank you and thrive given the growing conditions that terrariums offer. Although I couldn't possibly list all of the players that don't love this particular field, there are general traits that just won't work in a terrarium.

Of course, there are size restrictions. Big plants will outgrow a terrarium rapidly. You can always put something that will grow large in a terrarium temporarily while it's still petite, keeping in mind that it'll need a promotion when it begins to move into the plus sizes. But to be foresighted (and to save yourself some hassle), you might as well go for a long-term relationship and avoid working with plants that are bound to rapidly overflow their bounds.

Light requirements will also limit your playing field. Cacti and succulents can never work in a terrarium. Geraniums, pelargoniums, herbs (except perhaps mints), bougainvilleas—anything that dotes on direct sun—isn't going to endure a terrarium. The fact that light levels won't support their flowers is only part of the constraint; they actually demand more sunbeams than you can furnish comfortably enclosed in glass. Save them for a brighter venue.

The name of the game in a terrarium is moisture and high humidity, which isn't every plant's preferred atmosphere. Certain plants favor the dampness in a terrarium, and they're nearly always tropical or fond of woodlands. Other plants will rot or fall victim to fungus. They won't be happy, or at least not for long. Since the idea is to create a thriving environment, choose plants that will live happily ever after in a terrarium. There are plenty of options!

A few of the groups of plants that won't work in a terrarium are:

Cacti

Succulents

Alpines

Most rock-garden plants

Pelargoniums

Herbs

Tolmeia menziesii—piggyback plant

Viola odorata 'Rosea'

conversation piece. Plus, it likes shade and thrives in a terrarium. And talk about an easy plant to propagate—this is Propagation 101. Just take off those plantlets and nestle them into the soil; they'll form roots and start a family of their own.

Violas—Violets

Most violets are perfectly happy living in a terrarium, and they have such a strong association with ferny dells and the like that they are a favorite for that function. Universally recognized and beloved, violets bring the outdoors inside. The only problem is that most true violets prefer cool temperatures to blossom. Not only do they cease to blossom, but they tend to get infested with red spider mites when their environment heats up. So most violets are best kept outdoors where it's cool and shady in the summer months. However, you could bring a cloche or lantern cloche outdoors and sequester a violet under glass in the shade, the cloche simply an ornamental accent. A terrarium could also protect a violet from frost and prolong its blooming performance in spring and autumn. In fact, the nonhardy Parma violets were once commercially grown under cloches to protect them from heavy frost.

Or, you might try a tender violet—such as *Viola hederacea*, the Tasmanian violet. It blossoms all the time—throughout the year—and it's fond of terrariums. Unlike typical shrinking violets, it holds its pert purple and white flowers above the leaves. It will roam and send little plantlets rooting around. But that just means there's more to share with terrarium-loving friends.

projects

NOW THAT YOU HAVE THE DESIRE TO BEGIN CREATING YOUR OWN SMALL WORLD, AND YOU'VE GOT THE KNOWLEDGE TO get started and an overview of what will work inside a glass case, you're undoubtedly wondering where this will lead you. What can you do with a terrarium? What functions can a terrarium perform for you? Here are some projects that will bring a terrarium into reality for you.

Sure, a terrarium is an intriguing concept. And certainly, a terrarium could simply provide something uplifting to behold for your edification indoors. But beyond just a pretty face, terrariums have further applications. They can delineate a convenient and confined space for you to profile favorite things from nature. They might spotlight prominent pieces from your collection of antiques. Or terrariums can protect something precious from danger or disaster at the hands of fast-moving children. On the other hand, they could enter into a childhood experience, hosting a child's little fantasy world where everything is scaled down. Or they can serve as an ode to a season with the finest finds from spring, summer, fall, or winter proudly displayed. A terrarium can be a business tool to give the public a hint of what you do professionally— a three-dimensional calling card, if you will—or it can act as a centerpiece. Terrariums can be totally fun and offbeat, and they can provide a tableau that makes even the most mundane objects memorable.

There's plenty that you can do with terrariums. And here are a few suggestions to get you started.

A SEASON CAPTURED: SPRING

PREVIOUS PAGE With a calling card enclosed, a terrarium can promote a craft. OPPOSITE A terrarium can include a garden scene in miniature ("gardener" included); the "palm tree" is a peperomia.

In the best of all springs, there would be scant call for a terrarium. If everything in life went according to plan, the weather would thaw and then spring bulbs would soldier on through a few chilly nights to blossom cheerfully in the garden on schedule. But the ideal doesn't always happen. There's that inevitable late-season snowstorm, burying all your treasures, obliterating the headway that all those misguided snowdrops and crocuses accomplished. This is the place where cloches traditionally came in.

Long before cloches became popular in our living rooms, they had a life outside. For centuries, gardeners pushed the seasons and protected their plants outdoors with glass cloches to moderate extreme temperatures and shelter tender sprigs from the cruel elements. If a few precocious fritillarias were fool enough to break ground in a warm spell followed by a spate of nasty weather, they were clapped within cloches to prevent frostnip. Cloches were an indispensable tool in an unstable world. Zonal denial has been a constituent of spring since time began, and cloches were conspirators in the folly.

Today, unless you're coddling a rare, questionably hardy snowdrop in the hinterlands of northern New York State (and, of course, I have just such a hopeless specialist in mind, and he uses plastic cloches for that purpose), your spring interactions with terrariums will most likely be indoors and of the aesthetic kind. Rather than fending off bitter chills,

you'll be creating a display case for a season's jewels—a vital endeavor of a different kind.

In spring, glass cases can be lifesavers. They definitely enhance the seasonal experience. Think about it. Much of spring's beauty and bounty is minuscule, nestled close to the ground, and best admired on hands and knees in the garden. Instead of shivering your way through nature, feeling your fingers going numb, why not bring the bounty inside? You could force some chionodoxas, snowdrops, or scillas by planting pots in autumn, chilling them in the refrigerator for eight weeks or so, and then putting them in a cloche or terrarium for your ultimate edification. Or pick up some preforced bulbs at the supermarket. There you have it— spring's glory at close quarters. In truth, those spring bulbs would be fine without high humidity or fussing. But then again, they're stunning when placed within a cloche. Suddenly a tiny little puschkinia is elevated to superstardom. In a setting all its own, that little bulb commands a closer look.

Not all forced bulbs last long within glass. Scilla blossoms linger per-fectly happily, but snowdrops need fresh, preferably nippy, air. A dinner party or a very brief debut is all that snowdrop flowers will endure enclosed in glass. But that quick detour does the bulbs no harm. Snow-drops should be transplanted while still green and growing, so a side trip into a terrarium can be part of their move or division. However, other spring bulbs will last longer. Glory-of-the-snow, lily-of-the-valley, and wood hyacinth linger many weeks, providing an absolutely thrilling interlude. There might be more to spring than bulbs, but they're a big part of the excitement.

You might pick up some of the other nonbulbous harbingers of spring to profile under glass. Primroses, lungwort, sea thrift, dwarf Solomon's seal, and dwarf bleeding hearts come to mind immediately, but other shade-loving heralds of spring are certainly options. Bringing them indoors and displaying them under glass gives you a taste of the season, while pushing the normal cycle into a faster pace. If spring is when every-one hungers for blossoms, then a terrarium quenches that craving with a magical spin. And, given the fact that spring always feels a little like a sus-pension of reality, terrariums fit right in.

This ode to spring under glass includes white wood hyacinth (right) and lily-of-the-valley with glory-of-the-snow (left).

A SEASON CAPTURED: SUMMER

Terrariums make it possible to get a little piece of summer anywhere and pretty much anytime. Many vestiges of summer will survive enclosed in glass. In fact, some of the quintessential components of the season can be tucked into terrariums to follow you whenever you need a dose of summer.

Take hostas, for example. For shade gardeners, hostas say summer. And the dwarf varieties are ideal for terrariums. Or try lamiums. You could pick up some of those handsome little creepers with intriguingly patterned foliage and pert flowers and they'd do just fine in a terrarium. The same is true for liriopes, hardy ferns (painted ferns are particularly riveting), tiarellas, heucheras, heucherellas, periwinkles, lamb's ears, and mints—to give just a sampling.

Since terrariums soften the boundaries between in and out, they can act as transitional elements on a screened porch. Use them as a segue, let them make the leap between your domain and outdoors. As a focal point on a porch, a terrarium says volumes, giving the sense of having one foot out the door—without the bugs. Again, monitor terrariums periodically to make sure that the glass case isn't sitting in the sun's direct path.

When your outdoor summer garden is in full swing, remember that terrariums aren't only for inside use. It's entirely possible to incorporate a terrarium or cloche into a garden outdoors. They perform the same task they provide inside, but in reverse. Cloches introduce the human element into an outdoor scene. They streamline the jagged edges of nature and tame it. They act as a window to what is wild. And they add a little sparkle where everything is earthy. Cloches and terrariums can become an unexpected focal point outdoors; they can serve as a piece of artwork that's uniquely personal. There will be very few concerns if your terrarium is a showpiece for lichen-patterned twigs and similar woodland treasures. However, bringing a glass case with plants outside requires some initial testing of the waters. Shade is critical. Half an hour of direct sun on a closed cloche outside can bake the contents beyond salvage— think of a closed automobile, and you've got a similar situation. Even in the shade, on a steamy summer day, the contents might heat up. A sealed terrarium—such as a cloche—should be tipped open (set the rim up on

This synthesis of summer couples seashells and beach glass with a potted heuchera.

bricks or terra-cotta "feet") to allow air movement. Needless to say, you want to concoct something stable—one strong gust and a cloche set askew can topple, with disastrous results.

Although you should take care with permanent outdoor terrarium installations, there are a few instances when you can toss caution to the wind. Suppose you're throwing a party and you need a centerpiece for a wedding, for example, or maybe a midsummer night's feast, or perhaps just a family picnic. If you want something personal and something that distills the moment, try a terrarium. You could compose a cloche with tiny bits from your home displayed within. A big bell jar with a tropical lady's slipper orchid holding forth makes a riveting tabletop focal point. Plant a sizable terrarium, use it as a centerpiece, and it becomes a conversation starter, hands down. If the event is being held outdoors for several hours during the day, you still need to shelter whatever is inside from direct sun if you hope to keep the contents alive. And if the event is being held inside, a terrarium incorporates the outdoors into the festivities. And, compared with a flower arrangement, a terrarium is much easier to compose. Not only is the project less daunting, but, unlike a flower arrangement, a terrarium can be pulled together in advance. Plus, the whole display will probably cost a fraction of the expense of cut flowers.

You can also take a more utilitarian tack with terrariums. In summer, terrariums can add an alluring accent, but they can also earn their keep. When you're starting seeds, you can use a terrarium to help the process along. For the germination process, terrariums furnish an ideal ecosystem for flowers or vegetables. A terrarium raises the humidity and also keeps temperatures warm and cozy while seeds are sprouting. As with most seed-starting rigs, terrariums are purely temporary quarters for seedlings. When those fleglings are up and running, you can easily lift, divide, repot, or transplant them to their future homes. Most vegetables won't survive long in a humid, confined terrarium, and certainly pollination would be inhibited by the glass. But when almost any plant is germinating, the terrarium acts as a facilitating tool.

Terrariums can serve another function, too. They can plant-sit. At a weekend house, you can tuck plants into a terrarium indoors without worrying about their watering needs during the week.

When you go on vacation, leave your plants safely under glass. You can be absent for weeks without pangs of guilt if your plants are sequestered within cloches, lanterns, or other terrariums. For a temporary gig such as a summer vacation, you might try putting plants that aren't generally terrarium-appropriate within glass to quell their thirst. You'll want to pull them away from direct light, even if they're normally sun lovers. But a week out of bright light certainly won't harm most plants.

However you play it, a terrarium can be a lifesaver in summer. When the outdoors is in leaf, and nature is going gangbusters, a terrarium can give you a little sampling of something that's generally a vicarious experience. Terrariums can cosset the sweetness of summer, distilled into a quick encounter.

A SEASON CAPTURED: AUTUMN

Autumn can be bittersweet. If your heart belongs outdoors, if you've spent the previous season interacting with the land as often as possible, or even if you've just slipped out for a walk in the park as frequently as time allows, then summer's end can be difficult to bear. This is a time when terrariums can help the most. A terrarium can ease the transition from summer to fall and stifle your homesickness for the outdoors. If ever there's an instance when terrariums come to your rescue, autumn is that moment. In a way, terrariums are just another manifestation of the urge to squirrel summer's bounty safely away for future enjoyment.

Terrariums provide practical services to shift into the shorter-day, colder-climate configuration. The transition from outdoors to inside can

Cookie jars can serve as venues to display the dried hydrangeas, bittersweet, rosehips, and fallen leaves of autumn.

be tricky for a plant. Be it annual, perennial, tropical, or native, one day that little plant is out basking in the humidity and moisture outdoors, and the next day it's being blasted by your furnace. The typical home tends to offer about as much humidity during the heating season as your average desert, which can be tough on plants *and* people.

A terrarium can counteract the effects of the furnace while a plant adjusts. Although something botanical may not want or need a terrarium in the long run, it might appreciate an enclosure that helps the transition. And many plants, such as miniature coleus, are suitable to stay in a glass enclosure for an extended period of time, affording a fitting testimony to the season gone by.

Enlist terrariums to do outdoor duties, too. Just as terrariums protected plants in the garden in spring, they can serve the same purpose in autumn. Outdoors, the coleus that will never endure frost, the tender miniature basil, and all the other easily frost-struck players of summer might have the potential of surviving many more weeks in the garden if they're protected from a light frost. Clap a cloche or terrarium over tender garden plants on chilly autumn nights, and you can extend their growing season. But don't forget to remove the covering when the sun shines later in the day—again, a cloche or closed environment can heat up rapidly. A cloche does the most mundane tasks with style, and it's definitely the high-profile way to approach protecting plants.

Accessing autumn's ingredients, two young naturalists use a terrarium as their artistic canvas.

You might want to go more low-tech outside, and you also might want to tighten the budget, especially if a slew of plants need protection. Expand your definition of the term *terrarium* to include a hotcap for the purpose of protecting tender plants. For that matter, a large vase will work in a pinch—and it can have similar panache to a cloche or something much more expensive.

With the help of a terrarium, autumn won't feel so dismal. By putting the emphasis on the sweet side of this bittersweet moment, fall can take on a more upbeat spin. In fact, with a terrarium waiting to be filled, fall can be the beginning of something beautiful.

A SEASON CAPTURED: WINTER

When you need nature most, terrariums can add green to your world. With the help of glass, you can have botany at your elbow in any weather, both day and night. In winter, terrariums can accompany you through the long, dark evenings and serve as a reminder that nature is out there waiting to be reborn.

Winter poses a few variables that aren't encountered during other seasons of the year. Depending on the weather in winter, monitoring might be wise while you're hitting your stride with terrarium growing. Naturally, it's prudent to get a feeling for the growing conditions in your home as the seasons swing around. Because winter is infamous for its extremes, a terrarium can be a learning experience. Be attentive to your terrarium as winter evolves.

In the cycle of the seasons, winter tends to be the wild card for indoor gardeners. Certainly, it offers a different set of parameters than other seasons. And terrariums might also entail some additional vigilance. You might need to ventilate or leave a case closed when the heat goes on. It will definitely be essential to move terrariums off radiators as soon as the heating season begins. But it might also be necessary to move a terrarium away from the fireplace. However, when you grow in a terrarium, humidity will be increased for the occupants, and that's a blessing in winter. With a terrarium, you've got a buffer between the dry climate of central heat (or, even worse humidity-wise, the parched heat of a woodstove or toasty blazing fireplace) and whatever living thing you might be nurturing within glass.

In winter, when light levels are low, you might want to push a terrarium closer to the windowpanes than its summer location. During long bouts of dreary weather or if you have low light levels in your house, apartment, or office, some supplemental light from a fluorescent lamp might be appreciated for plants other than ferns and lovers of very low light.

As far as care is concerned, you might have to provide occasional supplemental water in cases that aren't sealed. Or, if you watered too heavily initially, you might need to drain the bottom of jars that you've planted directly in to keep their moss fresh. Beyond that, a terrarium is pretty much on its own—and that's the point. But that said, you should keep tabs

Wintergreen *Gaultheria procumbens*, lingers longer under glass.

on your terrarium. Paying attention is bound to be one of the season's more delightful duties. Can you think of anything more cheering than pondering a small world of greenery when there's a blizzard outside?

A winter terrarium can be your salvation. It might help fend off seasonal affective disorder or mitigate the winter blahs. Just thinking of something green and happening can forestall all types of seasonal depression. It's certainly worth a try.

COSSETING COLLECTIONS

The plant world is particularly fertile ground for anyone with an innate penchant toward collecting. You could, of course, just start amassing a totally arbitrary assemblage of plants. Or you could focus. And if a terrarium is part of your life, zeroing in on a specific group of plants becomes much easier. You can concentrate your collecting efforts on one of the many groups of plants that enjoy the glass venue. Not only will you have the perfect place to profile a collection of plants, but your chances of success are heightened, thanks to your glass enclosure.

Housing a group with many shared preferences makes tending a terrarium easier. First of all, the members are likely to dwell in peace and harmony. Stick with a single collection when planting a terrarium, and policing won't be such a critical issue. But furthermore, everything dwelling within the terrarium is likely to have the same set of needs and requirements. Your worries about providing for each individual plant and its desires will be alleviated.

All these tillandsias share similar growing requirements.

When you compose a compote of flame violets (episcias), they make easy bedfellows.

There are design-related advantages to collecting as well. When you compose a collection, you have an immediate set of things that work well together, aesthetically speaking. Not only are all the plants in a group apt to favor similar growing conditions, but their similarities make them display nicely side by side. Like a family portrait where the members tend to reflect well on each other, plants are also harmonious.

So, when you compose a terrarium filled with plants that share characteristics, you already have a common vocabulary. Since you're designing in a very confined space, the inherent harmony of the occupants can help in establishing mutual ground and it can prevent confusion from too many disparate entities. A collection can have a recurring theme that might serve as a motif in close quarters. Of course, you'll need some contrast to punch up the picture. But most plant families are sufficiently diverse to make the picture highly defined and riveting.

There are infinite arguments to recommend making a collection and giving it the glint of glass. In a nutshell, thinking *inside* the box is a way to exhibit a collection and allow it to dwell conveniently close by. Terrariums offer a sterling opportunity to sharpen your observational tools, and watch your collection grow.

MEMENTOS

One of the best parts of traveling is going somewhere that offers the opportunity to bring home meaningful bits from your trip. Some people might buy souvenirs when they journey. However, if you're a certain type of person, you don't find your most momentous mementos in shops; instead, the tokens are taken from the pathways you traveled. Maybe it's a curly shred of birch bark or a seedpod that you've never seen before. If you toss your newfound treasures on a shelf when you get home, they'll be lost in the shuffle. But put them in a glass jar, and they're promoted to pieces of art and your best memories are on display.

So, how do you start cosseting your mementos in a terrarium? A good place to begin would be to set the stage. When you're gathering pieces of nature, you need to bring them all to a common ground. Sheet moss can do that; it speaks the same vocabulary as all the other elements of the earth. Spread sheet moss on the floor of your terrarium or jar, and the green carpet foundation lays one texture in place to launch your saga in feathers, honeycomb, twigs, bark, or whatever else.

A starfish and coral give glitz to your home decor.

Of course, not all your mementos will be from the forest. The globe is punctuated by different habitats, wet and dry. If the seashore or the desert is your focus, pebbles and sand can serve the same function as the moss backdrop, providing mutual turf for seashells, starfish, or the like (all should be collected ethically and cleaned properly, of course). With that background, you're showing the relationship between all your valuables; you're establishing a link, allowing them to relate.

Once you've set the background, you can take it from there. The options are endless; building a collection of artifacts under glass is so highly personal, there are no rules. Parameters are inflicted only by the object you're filling—the glass area sets space guidelines, and those are the boundaries. But besides that criterion, the contents are open-ended. You're free to follow your own drummer.

Think about using the entire space available when you're designing a showcase for treasures. If you have a tall, lean cloche, for example, consider giving the eye something to follow vertically upward. Long shreds of fungi-dappled bark can serve that function—and, of course, taking bark from a dead, decaying tree does no harm. Upright twigs also efficiently fill a vertical space, giving the display depth and dimension, making it feel real. Horizontal spaces aren't challenging, but laying shells or intriguing stones on the floor of a terrarium gives your eye a path to follow.

Terrariums traditionally have connections with the earth. Nature is a perfect fit for terrariums, but other treasures can work under glass as well. The memento medium can take on many guises, and terrariums act as showcases no matter what your bent happens to be. If you've been amassing antique carpentry tools, old pencil sharpeners, piggybanks, bits of broken china, or sea glass, here's where you can put them. Why not compose a three-dimensional collage? The sheet music from your first date, the faux flowers from your wedding cake—whatever is important to you, it can all come together under one glass enclosure. Avoid combining moss or moisture-producing elements with humidity-sensitive treasures. Your composition will accent the interplay of textures, colors, and shapes, but it also represents the fabric you've woven of your life. In the end, what you compile in this very personal terrarium is less of a collection and more of a creation. Plus, it becomes a valuable sharing tool.

ABOVE Shells are given a shine in a terrarium. **OPPOSITE** To remind you of your beach and forest vacations, stash your treasures under glass.

A MINIATURE LANDSCAPE

If you've always wanted a garden, a terrarium can be a succinct landscape waiting to happen. With a Wardian case or sizable glass aquarium at your command, virtually any style of gardening is possible. You can literally design a garden condensed into a couple of feet (or less) of space. Of course, everything will have to be diminished in size, but that's part of the pleasure of planting a scene inside a terrarium.

A garden in glass follows all the same rules as any type of landscape, large or small. You'll want to consider all the facets of design that govern what you grow outdoors. But of course, everything is downsized. Part of the fun is finding plants that mimic the trees, shrubs, perennials, vines, and ground covers outdoors. All the elements in a landscape can come into play—including hardscape, contours, structures, and paths. Creating a miniature landscape accesses all your resources, but it also gives a tremendous sense of accomplishment.

The first step toward creating a miniature garden scene is to find a venue with sufficient space to make it happen. You should choose a Wardian case with enough room to host a number of plants. Your design will also be facilitated if your Wardian case has a base that can hold soil. The deeper that base is, the easier it will be to work your magic. Even the tiniest plant plugs are rooted in an inch or more of soil. If your terrarium or Wardian case has a base that is 2 inches or deeper, you can make this work conveniently. If not, you can build a scene up with soil and stone, but building the soil strata above the base will prove to be more of a logistical problem when it comes to watering, maintenance, and so on. A base to plant within is always a good starting point.

Beyond that requirement, any terrarium is applicable, depending on what you're trying to achieve. If you're striving to portray a mini backyard, a condensed estate, or a small barnyard scene, then ample space is a strong criterion when selecting the right glass venue for the job. When you've found a suitable case, just follow the rules of garden design. As with all design, it's easiest if you have a solid object to design around, no matter how complex the undertaking. Your central object might be a tiny house, or it might be a gnome or a bonsai-size tree. It could even be a set of stones meant to serve as a mini meditation garden. Use that object, or

Create a cairn under glass and it's less likely to topple.

set of objects, as your frame of reference and work outward from there.

Outdoors, focal points would be set off by a walkway, cobblestones, ground covers, or perhaps grass. The same theory can be applied to miniature elements that play the same roles. Gravel can mimic paving, a mirror might be a pond. Certain plants can imitate lawn—miniature cymbalaria, moss, creeping fig, and miniature ajuga all work for covering ground. They help to offset the focal point and give it the space that will make it prominent.

Of course, that's just the beginning. Your scene can expand from there, depending on the space available. Employ plants that appear to be miniature trees such as upright peperomias or begonias, as well as shrubs-in-miniature such as impatiens and serissas. A *Malpighia coccigera* might be a miniature holly, a seedling pine might be a Christmas tree. You could use little tufts of carex to imitate iris or round-leaved begonias to look like someone shrank the elephant's ears. Climbing fern, ivy, cissus, or any other tiny-leaved, low-light-tolerant mini vine could scramble up a trellis. You're getting the picture.

Miniature furniture (benches, chairs, you name it) can certainly be part of the lilliputian landscape, and you could tuck in mini birdhouses, pergolas, birdbaths, or whatever. This crystal kingdom could be populated by elves, soldiers, grazing sheep, cows, or extraterrestrial aliens. There might be trouble in mini paradise—it might be invaded by metal bunnies or plastic deer or a prowling carved wood fox. Just keep in mind the practical factor that when you mix soil, plants, and objects, you should be concerned with rust and paint issues. Be sure that whatever you're using is waterproof, because it's bound to be damp.

The point is, there's no right or wrong approach here. Nothing about a terrarium is irrevocable. If you don't like your composition, you can fiddle with its facets, change it around, and replant it. It's a growing scene, so it might alter with maturity. Expect your composition to change. When it does, divide and/or reposition the plants; let the terrarium become your creative outlet.

CHILD'S PLAY

Given an elaborate Wardian case, some imagination, and kalanchoe flowers, you've got an instant florist's shop in miniature.

Terrariums are the perfect tool to educate children about plants—innumerable teachers have already taken that route. There's plenty of precedent for taking a terrarium, filling it with carnivorous plants, and watching them grow, much to the delight of anyone who's attracted to elements of nature that might be classified as slightly yucky. Similarly, there's nothing new about letting a terrarium house plants in a classroom to teach lessons about ecosystems. These employments are valid; they're classroom classics, and completely within the typical terrarium/teaching realm. But you could also just take a glass case and some plants and let a kid have a ball—no restrictions, no expectations, no prompting—and learning will come from doing.

Think about tree houses, forts, secret hideaways, or whatever else you'd call a kid's own personal space. The wonder that kids glean from delineating their own domain is the same sort of wonder that they get from a terrarium. The same magnetism that draws kids to tree houses also attracts them to terrariums. Every kid yearns to create a fantasy world all their own. It's the wonder of minutiae, it's the illusion of magic, and

it's the draw of the surreal that attracts children to these venues. Kids relate to the smallness of it. Remember your youth, and think about what sparked your ingenuity. Maybe it was giants, but it was probably also elves and the miniature world they inhabited that jump-started the wheels of your creativity.

A terrarium introduces fantasy into a child's world. With a few forays into the woods, a child can return home with all the fixings for his or her fantasy terrarium. Be sure to go along for the collecting spree to make sure your child doesn't remove anything from nature that will deplete the natural stores. In fact, this is a good opportunity to discuss the whole concept of endangered species and woodland ethics. (And you'll be there to discourage collecting abandoned bird's nests and other things that should remain untouched, including poison ivy!) Left to their own devices, chil-

dren will come up with all sorts of organic glitz that you never noticed before. Pebbles, twigs, pods, fallen leaves, and the rest of nature's discards are treasures for children.

When you get home, set up a simple terrarium venue for your child and let her or him create magic with the treasures just acquired. Kids will love to arrange their treasures and create a world for little people. Plus, the contents are protected from bungling toddling siblings and the wagging tails of pets. Less wreckage, less heartbreak.

Creating a terrarium with a child is a perfect excuse to take a walk in the woods together. It's a reason to look, see, find, and fetch what you discover. Once children have collected all those goodies, they can use their artistic creativity to create a simple glass kingdom. The results might not be polished, but your child's imagination will be ignited.

MULTIPLICATION

Gardeners are always tempted to increase their bounty. If you've got one coleus, you could definitely use two. Or, thinking of it from the practical standpoint, propagation is the safe way to ensure that the plants you grew last season will grace your garden next year. Propagating your own plants is thrifty, but it's also smart and prudent. Terrariums can aid and abet your scheme to multiply the goods.

That's where a cloche or Wardian case comes in. Most cuttings fail because they wilt. In need of a constantly moist environment, they become stressed and fall victim to a fungus—or they just shrivel up and call it quits. A terrarium comes to the rescue. It keeps the plant's humidity level high while also maintaining moist underpinnings. As a result, not only is the process easier, it's more apt to be successful. Roots might even form more rapidly in a terrarium, especially with the help of rooting hormone—a compound that speeds up the root-forming process for a cutting (see page 161). Fast-rooting plants are a cinch in a terrarium. But you can also try propagating plants that might be more difficult to root—such as woody plants.

LEFT A creeping Charlie cutting gets a head start in a glass bowl. **OPPOSITE** Given the glass enclosure that it demands, the rhizomatous begonia 'Rajah' sends down roots and thrives to produce a flower.

Different plants take more or less time to establish roots. A coleus can root in a matter of days. A woody plant, such as a camellia, will take longer. So different plants will be sequestered in their propagation chamber for varying durations. But there's virtually no fuss while the rooting process is in action—except for checking the cutting occasionally to make sure that its soil isn't dry.

You can save yourself a fortune by using a terrarium for rooting. And you can also secure a plant that you've always hungered to grow. Plus, it's a riveting diversion to preoccupy a gardener when you might not be able to go outside. Be frugal and multiply.

Miniature impatiens aren't difficult to root, but a cloche streamlines—and quickens—the process.

RECUPERATION

You're not the only one who can reap the benefits of a terrarium. If you happen to have a plant that is doing poorly, this might be just the interlude that it needs to go green again. A terrarium can serve as a convalescent unit where plants can mend. It can be a temporary healing chamber when a plant is feeling the effects of stress. Or it might just furnish a halfway house between outdoors and indoors.

A terrarium provides a stable environment that moderates stress and gives plants the respite they need to recover. Transition can be tough on a

When a little dicentra from the garden is looking wan, give it a cloche to speed its recovery.

plant. No matter if it's going from outdoors to indoors, or moving from a greenhouse to a windowsill, climatic change can ruffle a plant. A terrarium is a stabilizing unit. It's like an oxygen tent for ailing plants. High humidity and even moisture serve as comfort food for most plants.

But be warned, a terrarium isn't always the answer. If a plant has mold, powdery mildew, a fungus, or a bacteria problem, a terrarium is likely to spread the blight rather than cure it. If a branch is partially broken off, it's not going to mend like a broken arm even though you've stashed the plant in a terrarium. And speaking of appendages, whatever the problem happens to be, you'd be wise to remove the affected parts before giving your plant the ER terrarium treatment. Blighted leaves will never become good again. Don't try to repot when something is looking sickly. Just put the plant in your recuperation chamber in its original container (by the same theory, leaving the patient in its pot is preferable to planting directly in a terrarium). Don't pour on the fertilizer, don't drench it with water. The last thing a plant needs when it's doing poorly is a feast.

Not everything wants to go the terrarium route when it's under the weather. Plants that like life dry and sunny won't respond—in other words, don't try this for desert plants. But any plant that hails from normally temperate regions is apropos. Nonetheless, don't overdo it. It's unwise to prolong therapy beyond the crisis time. When healing happens, whisk the plant out of the terrarium. Give it even moisture and strive to keep the humidity levels elevated during transition back into the fold. And try not to repeat the mistakes that led to decline.

Terrariums can tend to the injured in their time of need. And they nurse with panache. Even a sickly plant can look wonderful under a cloche, in a Wardian case, or in any other terrarium. It's part of the magic inherent to a glass world.

⟁

The goal for all these projects is to create something that flows into your lifestyle, no parameters, no reservations. You want your terrarium to look intuitive and feel unposed. When the goal is to tuck a terrarium into your home and make it feel unstudied, you might want to downplay a ter-

Put a terrarium in the heart of your home. There's nothing more peaceful than a sunbeam and a small world.

rarium rather than presenting it with the interior-decor version of a drumroll. Rather than setting it apart as a shrine, bring the terrarium into the throng. Rather than treating a terrarium like an honored guest, make it work with the scene. Put it next to the sofa, not off to the side in a lonely corner. Weave it in. When you've succeeded with terrariums, it becomes a habit. Your eye comes to expect it. That little bit of verdure has become essential. It's a given. And making the leap possible is what terrariums are really all about.

CASE STUDIES

Now you're undoubtedly wondering exactly how to go about planting a terrarium. You're ready for the precise step-by-step procedures to make this work for you. And just as with cooking or any other process, certain techniques will be more apt to result in a successful terrarium over the long haul. Other methods might also work, but here's how I plant a cloche, case, or bell jar. These are strategies that I find effective. And hopefully, they'll work for you, too.

Working with terrariums poses some unique challenges. Even if you've worked with plants all your life, the glass venue poses its own set of parameters that are similar to, but not quite the same as, those encountered in other gardening situations. And each type of terrarium has its own specific set of techniques that will help you to achieve success. Whether you're working with a bell jar, a cloche, or a Wardian case, if you follow certain steps, your composition is more likely to be effective and continue to function as it should over many weeks, months, and maybe even years.

Planting in Moss in a Jar

Many plants do perfectly well nestled in a bed of moss planted directly into a glass jar. With the moss lining the walls of the jar, it makes a handsome composition.

APPROPRIATE PLANTS

Miniature begonias

Gesneriads

Miniature orchids

Venus flytrap—*Dionaea*

Nerve plants—*Fittonia*

Waffle plant—*Hemigraphis*

Mosses

Dwarf ferns

INGREDIENTS

Jar, with or without a lid (apothecary jars and bell jars are also appropriate)

Charcoal pieces (from an aquarium supply shop or garden center)

Sheet moss

Potting soil

HELPFUL TOOLS

Gloves

Tongs or long-handled tweezers

Barbecue skewer with cork on tip

Watering can

METHOD

1. Choose a jar with or without a lid—any size will do, from Mason jar dimensions on up to larger apothecary jars and bell jars.

2. Select a plant to grow inside, taking into account the proportions of both plant and jar.

3. Sprinkle a thin layer of charcoal pieces into the bottom of the jar.

4. Wearing gloves, lay a carpet of sheet moss over the bottom and partially up the sides of the jar (tongs might be necessary if you can't fit your hand inside) until there's a soft bed of sheet moss where the plant's roots will sit—this will help to sponge up excess water.

5. Remove the plant from its container and tuck it into the moss bed (again, use tongs if you can't fit your hand into the jar).

Planting in Soil in a Jar

When you've got a plant that just wicks up moisture, it's possible to plant it directly in soil in a glass enclosure and watch it thrive. If a grass is what you're working with, you'll want to use a jar with an open top. For smaller plants, a jar with a lid is appropriate.

APPROPRIATE PLANTS

    Rhizomatous begonias

    Ornamental grasses

    Peperomias

INGREDIENTS

    Jar, with or without a lid

    Charcoal pieces (from an aquarium supply shop or garden center)

    Potting soil

HELPFUL TOOLS

    Gloves

    Tongs

    Long-handled, narrow trowel

    Barbecue skewer with cork on tip

    Watering can

METHOD

1. Wearing gloves, put a layer of charcoal into the bottom of the jar.

2. Mix well-drained soil with a sprinkling of charcoal and lay a bed of that soil on top of the charcoal, just as you would prepare any container to receive a transplant.

3. Remove the plant from its container and tuck it into the jar (tongs will help if the mouth of the jar is narrow).

4. Fill in the sides with soil, firming the soil down around the plant with the cork-tipped barbecue skewer.

5. Water very lightly.

6. Clean off the sides of the jar so you can get a clear window on the plant inside.

6. Add potting soil to fill in, if necessary, potting the plant into the moss bed as you would transplant into any container. Firm the soil in (a barbecue skewer fitted with a cork tip is helpful here).

7. Tuck the moss in over the soil of the new transplant and top-dress if there is exposed soil.

8. Water lightly.

9. Clean off the sides of the jar so you can get a clear window on the growing plant.

Putting a Potted Plant into a Jar, Aquarium, or Case

Rather than planting directly in a jar or case, you might want to pot a plant and put it inside a jar or case in its container. This is particularly effective with plants that need good drainage. It also gives you more control—you can easily lift the potted plant out for aeration if the container becomes too humid. In addition, you have more flexibility—it's easy to switch plants at whim. And you can also put several plants side by side in a sizable case. Needless to say, the container should be sufficiently narrow to fit through the mouth of the glass case. This sounds obvious, but give it a dry run before you actually repot—I've occasionally misjudged.

APPROPRIATE PLANTS

Any of the plants recommended in
Part 5: The Plants

INGREDIENTS

Jar or case of sufficient size for the target plant
Pebbles
Charcoal pieces (from an aquarium supply store or garden center)
Ornamental pot of any description, but of the proper proportions to fit
Potting soil or orchid medium
Topdressing material such as colorful stones, sheet moss, and the like (optional)

HELPFUL TOOLS

Gloves
Watering can

METHOD

1. Depending on the shape of the container, lay a bed of pebbles mixed with some pieces of charcoal on the bottom of the jar or case.

2. Select an ornamental pot that is the same size or one size larger than the pot in which the plant you plan to exhibit in your terrarium is currently growing. The pot that you choose should fit inside the jar or case without crowding (it will also have to fit through the door or opening of the jar—this can be a little trickier than the ship-in-the-bottle caper). Remember that the pot will be prominently displayed, and select accordingly.

3. Transplant your plant into the ornamental pot, taking care to firm the soil around the root ball. Leave sufficient space between the rim of the pot and the soil line to allow you to water.

4. Water the plant after potting, and cover with sheet moss or topdressing as you prefer.

5. Put the plant into the jar or case and monitor it, especially initially, to learn its watering needs, if any.

6. Water lightly, if watering is necessary.

Planting in a Pot Within a Cloche

There are a couple of ways to display plants within a cloche. By far the easiest method is to take a potted plant, preferably in a profile-worthy container, and set it within the cloche. No matter what you use, even the most modest plant will look tremendous in a showcase setting. Not only that, but this is a breeze (and extremely rewarding) for a beginner.

APPROPRIATE PLANTS

Rhizomatous begonias

Pitcher plants—*Sarracenia*

Venus flytrap—*Dionaea*

Ferns of all sorts

Gesneriads of all sorts

Mosses

Orchids

Peperomias

Many of the other plants mentioned in Part 5: The Plants

INGREDIENTS

Ornamental pot of any description, but of the proper proportions to fit

Potting soil or orchid medium

Sheet moss or pebbles for topdressing (optional)

Saucer for drainage

Waterproof charger, plate, or tray to serve as a bottom

Cloche that's sufficiently tall and wide to fit its resident plant without squeezing

HELPFUL TOOLS

Gloves (if using moss)

Watering can

METHOD

1. Repot your plant into the ornamental container, selecting a pot that is the same size as the pot it's currently in or not more than one or two pot sizes larger. If you prefer to keep your plant in its original plastic container (and that might be the easiest way to go for an orchid), tuck it into an ornamental cachepot.

2. Put a saucer beneath the plant, just in case—note that metal pots can cause rust stains beneath in the damp environment.

3. Put the saucer and its potted plant onto the charger, plate, or tray.

4. Water lightly and clamp the cloche on top.

Planting Directly in the Base of a Cloche

There are terra-cotta bases made specifically to suit cloches. They usually resemble a shallow saucer, often with a depth of only 2 inches or so to plant within. So manipulating the roots in such a shallow surface can be a challenge. Quite often a grouping of plants—maybe an orchid and a fern or a pitcher plant and a selaginella moss—are tucked in together, making for an evocative vignette. Here's how to accomplish the feat.

APPROPRIATE PLANTS

Rhizomatous begonias

Pitcher plants—*Sarracenia*

Ferns of all sorts

Gesneriads of all sorts

Mosses

Orchids

Creeping peperomias

INGREDIENTS

Potting soil or orchid medium

Terra-cotta cloche base (or substitute a deep saucer)

Sheet moss for topdressing (optional)

Waterproof charger, plate, or tray to prevent damage to furniture

Cloche that's sufficiently tall and wide to fit its resident plant without squeezing

HELPFUL TOOLS

Gloves

Watering can

METHOD

1. Lay a shallow layer of soil and/or moss on the bottom of the base (wear gloves when dealing with moss).

2. Choose a focal-point plant to place toward the center. If you're working with an orchid, remove it from its pot and spread out the roots.

3. Add soil or orchid medium around the roots.

4. Add a fern or companion plant if you like, also placed toward the center of the base. Tease the roots to lie horizontally if the plant's original container is deeper than the receptacle.

5. Fill in with orchid medium or soil, depending on what you're growing, making sure to cover the roots. Mounding might be necessary—this shouldn't be a problem because, after the initial watering, the high humidity will lessen the need to water.

6. Level the soil around the edge where the glass of the cloche will sit so it's a flat surface.

7. Top-dress with sheet moss, if desired (don't use pebbles, as that would result in an unsteady foundation for the cloche).

8. Water lightly, place on the charger, plate, or tray, and cover with the cloche.

Planting Directly in a Wardian Case (or Aquarium)

Wardian cases are often solidly glazed or two-part units with a frame for the glass (like a greenhouse) and a waterproof base (sometimes it's metal, sometimes it's metal with a plastic liner, sometimes it's zinc) deep enough to plant in. This configuration is the most convenient and flexible for planting purposes. The deeper the base, the more you can pack in. With a 3-inch base, you can easily entertain mature plants, if the case has sufficient headroom. A Wardian case with a plantable base is the ideal format for creating a miniature scene. Here's how it's done.

APPROPRIATE PLANTS

Rhizomatous begonias

Ferns of all sorts

Gesneriads of all sorts

Mosses

Orchids

Peperomias

Pileas

Air plants (these can just hang around, no planting necessary)

All of the other plants mentioned in Part 5: The Plants

INGREDIENTS

Wardian case with a watertight base sufficiently deep to be planted in

Waterproof tray (even though the base is watertight, leaks can happen)

Pebbles or gravel

Charcoal pieces (from an aquarium supply store or garden center)

Potting soil

Sheet moss or pebbles for topdressing (optional)

Ornaments to give your scene its personality, such as little houses, toy soldiers, little people, action figures, toy animals, toy cars, and whatever else you fancy (optional)

HELPFUL TOOLS

Gloves

Tongs

Barbecue skewer with cork on the tip for firming the soil

Watering can

METHOD

1. Spread an inch of pebbles or gravel (¼- to ½-inch is best) on the bottom of the case.

2. Wearing gloves, sprinkle in charcoal pieces and mix with the pebbles.

3. Add a layer of potting soil to the depth of the planting tray or base. Usually 2 inches of soil will be sufficient to cover most small plants.

4. Smooth the soil over, firming it to create a clean, flat planting bed (just like the bed you'd create for a garden, but scaled down).

5. Remove the plants from their containers, tease a few roots free if they're pot-bound, and tuck them into the soil by digging small holes to receive them.

6. Firm each plant in after planting. This is

important, as air pockets can lead to trouble in a terrarium just as they would in the garden.

7. Place on waterproof tray and water the plants lightly in their new home.

8. Add stones and other ornamental features.

9. Monitor your small world to make sure everything is coexisting happily.

Planting in Containers in a Wardian Case with Removable Glass Panes

Some Wardian cases have panels of glass rather than being fitted with glass glazed into a frame. Due to the air spaces between the panes, they aren't airtight (hint: If you hear rattling when you carry your Wardian case around, it's probably got glass panels). As a result of the air spaces, humidity might not be as high as in an airtight case, so keep an eye on humid-loving plants. One symptom of humidity stress on a plant is shriveling and curling of the leaf edges. Because this type of Wardian case usually doesn't have a plantable base, it's wisest to exhibit the plants in their containers. No problem, but remember to monitor for moisture and water occasionally, if necessary. And also keep a watchful eye for water buildup in the bottom. Water leakage is more likely to be an issue outside of this case as well. Here's how to handle the venue.

APPROPRIATE PLANTS

Rhizomatous begonias

Ferns of all sorts

Gesneriads of all sorts

Carnivorous plants

Mosses

Orchids

Peperomias

Pileas

Air plants (these can just hang around, no planting necessary)

Many of the other plants mentioned in Part 5: The Plants

INGREDIENTS

Wardian case

Pebbles or gravel

Charcoal pieces (from an aquarium supply store or garden center)

Waterproof base (leaks are apt to happen)

Ornamental pots

Saucers to collect water under the plants (if the base is not watertight)

Potting soil

Sheet moss or pebbles for base or topdressing

HELPFUL TOOLS

Gloves

Watering can

METHOD

1. To elevate the humidity when planting in a Wardian case that has removable glass panes, put a 1-inch layer of pebbles or gravel mixed with charcoal pieces on the bottom of the base, if a base is available.

2. If it's watertight, pour a thin layer of water into the base. If excess water builds up when you're caring for the plants, be sure to drain it when necessary and monitor for leakage.

3. Put your pots in containers on top of this base.

4. If your case does not have a watertight base, with gloves on, spread sheet moss on the floor of the base to raise the humidity.

5. This venue will dry out more frequently than most types of terrariums. Check the soil of the pots for moisture often and water if necessary.

Using a Jar, Case, or Aquarium for Cuttings

One of the functions that a terrarium can provide is a stress-free chamber for propagating plants. Due to the elevated humidity, cuttings take root much more rapidly and with less trouble than they would in open air. You can root a cutting in a pot placed inside the terrarium, or root directly in a layer of soil in the base if the terrarium has a watertight base. Indirect light is crucial when you're rooting cuttings—you don't want to stress a sprig with no roots by exposing it to bright light. But dark doesn't work either. Most cuttings can be rooted in this manner. However, the process will take longer for woody plants.

APPROPRIATE PLANTS

Almost any plant will work, as long as you can take cuttings

Begonias

Gesneriads

INGREDIENTS

Wardian case

Waterproof tray (leaks are apt to happen)

Small pots to root in (preferably smaller than 4 inches in diameter)

Propagation mix or coarse sand

Rooting hormone

Pebbles or gravel

Charcoal pieces (from an aquarium supply store or garden center)

Gloves

Pruners or scissors to take the cutting and
remove lower leaves

Knife to slit a hole in the soil to receive the cutting

Watering can

METHOD

1. Fill a small pot with a light propagation mix
(coarse sand is also a possibility, but you'll probably
need to supply additional water).

2. Take a tip cutting—in general a cutting should
be at least 2 to 3 inches long but not more than
4 inches in length.

3. Remove the lower leaves. If the leaves are large,
cut them in half to reduce transpiration stress.

4. Apply rooting hormone (a compound that
expedites the root-forming process) to the tip of the
bottom of the stem—don't overdo it, as too much
hormone is counterproductive. Shake off the excess.

5. Make a slit or hole (depending on the stem's
width) in the soil for the cutting and insert the
bottom one-third of the cutting into the slot.

6. Firm the soil around the stem.

7. Water lightly.

8. Put the pot with its cutting on a waterproof tray
and place into the case.

9. Monitor for signs of rooting—when a cutting is
rooted, it stands upright and begins to make
growth. If in doubt, tug gently on the stem. If the
cutting resists your pull, roots are probably
anchoring it down.

10. Alternative: Prepare the base of a Wardian case
as you would if you were planting directly in soil
with a layer of pebbles and charcoal, and then a
layer of soil (see page 165). Insert the cutting
directly into the base. If the cutting isn't destined to
dwell in the glass case over the long haul, you will
have to pot it into a container once it has rooted.

RESOURCES

Terrariums aren't hard to find. Once you're on the
lookout, you're likely to find cloches, apothecary jars,
canning jars, and vases everywhere you turn, including your local garden center, flea markets, garage
sales, and home goods stores, among other places.
If you think creatively, almost anything made of
glass can be enlisted. Here are a few of our favorite
sources for terrariums, terrarium supplies, and information. But this list is just a beginning; it is by no
means complete.

Terrariums

BLACK JUNGLE TERRARIUM SUPPLY
370 Avenue A
Turners Falls, MA 01376
800-268-1813

CAMPO DE' FIORI
1815 N. Main Street
Sheffield, MA 01257
www.campodefiori.com

CHRISTMAS TREE SHOPS
www.christmastreeshops.com

ELEISH-VAN BREEMS ANTIQUES
487 Main Street S.
Woodbury, CT 06798
www.evbantiques.com

ENGLISH CREEK GARDENS
800-610-8610
www.englishcreekgardens.com

THE FARMER'S DAUGHTER
Route 138
South Kingstown, RI 02892
401-792-1340
www.thefarmersdaughterri.com

GLASSHOUSE WORKS
P.O. Box 97
Church Street
Stewart, OH 45778-0097
740-662-2142
www.glasshouseworks.com

H. POTTER
www.hpotter.com

HOME GOODS
www.homegoods.com

MARIANI GARDENS
45 Bedford Road
Armonk, NY 10504
914-273-3083
www.marianigardens.com

NEW ENGLAND GARDEN ORNAMENTS, INC.
P.O. Box 235
38 East Brookfield Road
North Brookfield, MA 01535
508-867-4474
www.negardenornaments.com

PERGOLA
7 East Shore Road
New Preston, CT 06777
860-868-4769
www.pergolahome.com

POTTERY BARN
www.potterybarn.com

ANNE AND GARRETT ROWE
The Sugarplum
Wilmot, NH
413-528-1857

SMITH & HAWKEN
Washington Supply
Washington, CT
860-868-7395
1-800-940-1170
smithandhawken.com

SOMEWHERE IN TIME
52 Water Street
Wiscasset, ME
207-242-9263

TARGET
www.target.com

TERRAIN AT STYER'S
914 Baltimore Pike
Glen Mills, PA 19342
610-459-2400
www.terrainathome.com

TODD FARM ANTIQUES & FLEA MARKET
Rowley, MA
978-948-3300
www.toddfarm.com

WARD'S NURSERY AND GARDEN CENTER
600 Main Street
Great Barrington, MA 01230
413-528-0166

WEST ELM
www.westelm.com

Online Resources

www.amphibiancare.com
www.bradsbegoniaworld.com
www.ferns.com

Plants

BLACK JUNGLE TERRARIUM SUPPLY
370 Avenue A
Turners Falls, MA 01376
800-268-1813
Aquatic plants, terrarium plants

BROKEN ARROW NURSERY
13 Broken Arrow Road
Hamden, CT 06518
203-288-1026
www.brokenarrownursery.com
Sarracenias

DIETRICH GARDENS LLC
155 Main Street N.
Woodbury, CT 06798
203-266-4439
www.dietrichgardens.com
Potted spring bulbs, perennials, selaginellas, ferns

THE FARMER'S DAUGHTER
Route 138
South Kingstown, RI 02892
401-792-1340
www.thefarmersdaughterri.com
Begonias and terrarium plants

GLASSHOUSE WORKS
P.O. Box 97
Church Street
Stewart, OH 45778-0097
740-662-2142
www.glasshouseworks.com
Terrarium plants of all sorts

GLENDALE BOTANICALS AVAILABLE THROUGH METROPOLITAN
631 S. Main Street
Great Barrington, MA 01230
413-644-8868
Paphiopedilum orchids, ferns

J & L ORCHIDS
20 Sherwood Road
Easton, CT 06612
203-261-3772
www.jlorchids.com
Miniature orchids

JIMMY'S GREENHOUSES & FLORIST
680 Cook Hill Road
Danielson, CT 06239
860-774-2076
www.jimmysgreenhouses.net
Pilea, selaginella

LAURAY OF SALISBURY
432 Undermountain Road, Route 41
Salisbury, CT 06068-1102
860-435-2263
www.lauray.com
Orchids, gesneriads, begonias

LEXINGTON GARDENS
32 Church Hill Road
Newtown, CT 06470
203-426-3161
www.lexingtongardens.com
Begonias, tropical mosses, terrarium plants of all sorts

LOGEE'S GREENHOUSES
141 North Street
Danielson, CT 06783
888-330-8038
www.logees.com
Terrarium plants of all sorts

MOSS ACRES
303 Upper Woods Road
Honesdale, PA 18431
866-438-6677
www.mossacres.com
Hardy moss

NASAMI FARM
128 North Street
Whately, MA 01373
413-397-9944
www.newfs.org
Nursery-propagated wildflowers

**NEW ENGLAND WILDFLOWER SOCIETY AT
GARDEN-IN-THE-WOODS**
180 Hemenway Road
Framingham, MA 01701
508-877-7630
www.newfs.org
Nursery-propagated wildflowers

PECKHAM'S GREENHOUSE
200 W. Main Road
Little Compton, RI 02837
401-635-4775
Terrarium plants of all sorts

STICKS AND STONES FARM
20 Huntingtown Road
Newtown, CT 06470
203-270-8820
www.sticksandstonesfarm.com
Hardy moss

TERRAIN AT STYER'S
914 Baltimore Pike
Glen Mills, PA 19342
610-459-2400
www.terrainathome.com
Terrarium plants

Supplies

BLACK JUNGLE TERRARIUM SUPPLY
370 Avenue A
Turners Falls, MA 01376
800-268-1813
*Accent items, decorative wood and ornaments,
thermometers, meters*

HYDROFARM
www.hydrofarm.com
Fluorescent lights

MOSSER LEE
W6585 Highway O
Millston, WI 54643
715-284-2296
www.mosserlee.com
Sheet moss

SUPERMOSS PRODUCTS COMPANY
Santa Barbara, CA
www.supermoss.com
Preserved sheet moss

Organizations

AMERICAN BEGONIA SOCIETY
www.begonias.org

AMERICAN FERN SOCIETY
www.amerfernsoc.org

AMERICAN GESNERIAD SOCIETY
www.gesneriadsociety.org

AMERICAN ORCHID SOCIETY
www.aos.org

BROMELIAD SOCIETY INTERNATIONAL
www.bsi.org

**INDOOR GARDENING SOCIETY OF AMERICA,
METROPOLITAN NEW YORK CHAPTER**
www.indoorgarden.org

NEW ENGLAND CARNIVOROUS PLANT SOCIETY
www.NECPS.org

ACKNOWLEDGMENTS

THIS BOOK simply wouldn't have happened without the help of friends, family, and resources who generously opened their homes and shared their creativity with us. Space doesn't allow us to thank the many, many people who came to our aid. But we're particularly indebted to the folks at Clarkson Potter—Judy Pray, who patiently molded this book into shape; Ashley Phillips, who is her assistant par excellence; Amy Pierpont, who planted the first seeds of inspiration; Lindsay Miller; and all the other players at Potter. Our thanks to our agent, Colleen Mohyde of the Doe Coover Agency. Philip Norman, curatorial assistant at the Museum of Garden History in London, Anne Rowe of the Sugarplum, and Debra Queen were invaluable resources in the historical research of terrariums. Michael Riley was the willing and knowledgeable expert consulted for fluorescent light information. Many people opened their homes to us, most especially Sarah Boynton, Robin Cockerline, Robin Magowan and Juliet Mattila, Michele Mathews, Betsy Nestler, Sarah Partyka of the Farmer's Daughter, Anne Rowe of the Sugarplum, Kit and Marty Sagendorf, and Peter Wooster. We are particularly grateful to the children who came, enjoyed terrariums with us, and patiently endured the camera: they were Maya Bosco Schmidt (we'd also like to thank her father, Eric Schmidt) and Kayleigh and Ashley Mulhare (we're grateful to their mother, Becky Mulhare). Kit Sagendorf created some brilliant, whimsical, and artistic miniature scenes for us to photograph. Rob Girard shared several of his most artful plants to encase in glass. Tom Winn and Ken Frieling of Glasshouse Works conferred with us and sent plants for us to experiment with. Logee's Greenhouses was equally generous providing plants to serve as models. English Creek Gardens, Smith & Hawken at Washington Supply, Eleish-Van Breems Antiques, and Pergola shared their terrariums with us. Ray Baker furnished natural crafts made by his own hands and inspired by his colorful imagination. Laura Evans dug up her own spring bulbs to encase in crystal. Jody Clineff juggled film with infinite patience while also handholding her sister/photographer. Dennis Sega schlepped glass around without breakage and scarcely a complaint. And Stacy Sirk of Terrain at Styer's shared some of her boundless enthusiasm just when our strength was flagging.

INDEX

Page numbers in italics refer to photographs.

Acorus minima, 107
acrylic terrariums, 27, 52
Adiantum spp. (maidenhair ferns), *53*, 94
African violet family (gesneriads), 84, 97, 97–99, *98*
African violets (saintpaulias), 23, 27, *98*, 99
air plants (tillandsias), *8*, 89, 89–90, *141*
Ajuga reptans, 112–13, *113*
alpines, 55, 122
alsobias, 97–99, *142*
aluminum plant, 110
aphids, 81
apothecary jars, 22, 46, 60, *63*
aquariums, 17, 44–45, *44*, 60, 76, *123*, 146
    planting in, 163, 165–66
aquatic plants, 45, 76
artillery plant, 112
Athyrium filix-femina, 96
autumn:
    fallen leaves of, 11, 16, *135*
    sunlight in, 27
    terrariums in, *135*, 135–37, *136*

baby's tears, *51*, 120, *121*
bacterial infections, 79, 81, 158
bark, 11, *12*, 145
battery cases, 19, 46
beach glass, *131*
beach mementos, *69*, *131*, *143*, 145
    see also seashells
beakers, 19, 46
begonias, *19*, *21*, *22*, *41*, *43*, 57, 60, 62, 84, 86–88, *87*, *88*, 149, *154*
bell-glasses, see cloches
bell jars, 46, 60, 68, 75
Biophytum sensitivum, 113
bird's nests and eggs, faux, *14*, 19, *33*, *124*
bleach, 70
bowls, 11, 19, *44*, 84, *120*, *155*
bromeliads, 89–90, *91*
    tillandsias (air plants), *8*, 89, 89–90, *141*
bugleweed, 112–13, *113*

bulbs, see spring bulbs
butterflies, 32
button fern, 96

cacti, 55, 122
cake stands, *25*, 115
calatheas, 119
canning jars, 46
Cape primroses, 97, 99
caring for terrariums, 73–81
    cleaning glass, 70, *75*, 79, 81
    fertilizing, 76, 158
    monitoring, 74–75, 80–81, 138–40
    removing overgrown plants, 78–79, 100
    removing spent flowers and leaves, 79, 158
    see also ventilation; watering
carnivorous plants, 90–93, *92*
cat's tongue plant, 111
centerpieces, 133–34
charcoal, 67, *67*, 70
cheese plates, covered, 19, *144*
children, terrariums for, 137, 150–53, *151–53*
chiritas, *18*, *54*
cleaning glass, 70, *75*, 79, 81
cloches (bell-glasses), 11, *12*, 19, *19*, *25*, *28*, *29*, 36–39, *37*, *38*, *53*, *54*, *58*, *59*, *65*, *77*, *87*, *94*, *101*, *108*, *123*, *124*, *128*, *140*, *145*, *147*, *156*, *157*
    humidity in, 60
    knobs on, 39
    outdoor uses for, *126*, 130–33, *132*, 137
    planting in, 56, 62, 164–65
    plastic (hotcaps), 19, 39
    temperature fluctuations and, 52
    ventilating, 60, 78, 123, 133
    see also lantern cloches
club mosses, 100–102, *101*, *102*
codonanthes, *65*, 97
cold frames, 19, 32–35
coleus, *121*, 121, 137, 156
collections, 141–42
color, design and, 61, 62, 64
colored glass, 46

compotes, 60–61, 84, 92, *142*
cookie jars, 11, 46, *102*, *135*, *152*
coral, *143*
cork, *54*
creeping Charlie, *111*, 112, *155*
crowding, fungal problems and, 62
cryptanthus, 90
Crystal Palace, 40, 74
cubes, glass, *26*, *159*
Cuphea hyssopifolia, 113, 114
cuttings, propagating plants from, *133*, *155*, 155–56, *156*, 167–68
Cyanotis kewensis, 115
Cyperus spp., *106*, 107

davallias, 94–96
design principles, 61–66, 146–49
dicentras, *157*
Dionaea muscipula, 90–93
display cases, *14*, *32*, 32–35, *33*, *80*, *152*
drainage, 66–67, 76, 138
driftwood, 11
Drosera capensis (sundew), 90, 93
Dryopteris filix-mas, 40, 96

earth star, 90
episcias (flame violets), 97–99, *142*
explorers, plants collected by, 40

"feet," for ventilating cloches, 60, 78, *123*, 133
ferns, 11, 16, 27, *48*, *51*, *53*, 57, *59*, *65*, *72*, 93–96, *95*, 149
    button (*Pellaea rotundifolia*), 96
    footed (davallias, humatas, and polypodiums), *59*, 94–96
    hardy, 130
    heart (*Hemionitis arifolia*), *95*, 96
    maidenhair (*Adiantum* spp.), *53*, 94
    male (*Dryopteris filix-mas*), 40, 96
    nephrolepis, 17, *56*, 94
    Wardian cases and, 40, *43*, 93, *148*
fertilizing, 76, 158
fiber-optic grass, *105*, 107
fig, creeping (*Ficus pumila* cvs.), *113*, *115*, 117, *120*, 149
Fittonia spp., *117*, 117

flame violets, 97–99, *142*
flasks, 46, *141*
flowers, 84
   faded, 79
   gesneriads and, *97*, 97–99, *98*
fluorescent lights, 52, 138
forcing bulbs, 129
friendship plant, 111–12
frost, 52, 137
fungal infections, 62, 67, 68, 79, 81,
   122, 158
furniture:
   miniature, 69, *69*, 150
   protecting from moisture, 52, *54*

Gaultheria procumbens, 140
gesneriads (African violet family),
   84, *97*, 97–99, *98*
glasses, drinking, *8*, 46, *56*
glory-of-the-snow, *128*, 129
gloves, 67, 68
goblets, 46, *56*
grasses, ornamental, 27, 76, *105*,
   105–7, *106*
gravel, *see* pebbles or gravel
greenhouses, miniature, 19, 35, *109*,
   133, 136
   see also lantern cloches; Wardian
     cases
ground covers, 45, 59, 65, 110, 149

hand-glasses, *see* lantern cloches
Hawaiian heather, 113, *114*
heart fern, *95*, 96
heat, 50, 52, 130, 138
Hedera helix, 116, 117–18
Hemionitis arifolia, 95, 96
herbs, 55, 122
heucheras, 25, *131*
holly, miniature, 119, 149
hostas, 60, 130
hotcaps, 19, 39
Hoya lacunosa, 113
humatas, 94–96
humidity, 20, 27, 29, 60–61, 84–86,
   138, 155, 158
   lids and, 44–45, 46
   plant selection and, 55, 122
hurricane lamps, 46, *84*

impatiens, 62, 84, 118–19, 149, *156*
incandescent light, 27
insects:
   carnivorous plants and, 90–93

displays of, *19, 32, 34*
   infestations of, 80–81
Isolepsis cernua, 105, 107
ivy, *11,* 27, *72, 132,* 149
   Hedera helix, 116, 117–18

jars, *18, 19, 25,* 46, *48,* 95, 97, *128,*
   131, 144, 154
   apothecary, 22, 46, 60, *63*
   bell, 46, 60, 68, 75
   cookie, *11,* 46, *102, 135, 152*
   planting in, 68, 161–63
jewel orchids, 103
Juncus effusus, 106

lady fern, 96
lady's slipper orchids (paphiope-
   dilums), 47, 103, *104,* 133
lamiums, 130
landscapes, miniature, *114, 127, 139,*
   146–50, *153, 159*
lantern cloches (hand-glasses), *34,*
   35, 35–36, 60, *85, 88*
lanterns, 46, *84*
leaves:
   autumn, *11, 16, 135*
   yellowed or damaged, 79, 158
Ledebouria socialis, 118, 119
lids, humidity and, 44–45, 46
light, 27, 50, 52, 122
   artificial, 27, 52, 138
   in autumn, 27
   diffuse, *48, 51*
   magnified by glass, *39,* 52
   rotating terrariums and, 65, 79
   in winter, 138
lily of the valley, *128,* 129
liriopes, 130
Loudon, J. C., 35
Loudon, Jane, 35
Ludisia discolor, 103

maidenhair ferns, *53,* 94
maidenhair vines, *84,* 119–20
male fern, 40, 96
Malpighia coccigera, 119, 149
marantas, 119
martini glass, *8*
masdevallia orchids, *10*
mementos, *11,* 143–45, *143–45*
Mexican foxglove, 122
mildew, powdery, 158
miniature scenes, *114, 127, 139,*
   146–50, *153, 159*

moisture, 158
   judging, 75, 76, 77
   see also humidity; watering
mold, 74, 75, 158
monitoring terrariums, 74–75,
   80–81, 138–40
mosaic plant, 117
mosses, *11,* 15, 24, 27, 47, 52, 62,
   63, 67, 77, 100–102, *101,* 124,
   138, *148*
   club (selaginellas), 100–102, *101,*
     102
   dividing, 100
   planting in, 161–62
   sheet, lining terrariums with, 68,
     76, 143
moth orchids, 105
muehlenbeckias, *84,* 119–20

Neoregelia marmorata, 91
nephrolepis ferns, *17,* 56, 94
nerve plant, 117, *117*

orchids, 26, 29, 37, *38, 40,* 43, 57,
   62, 84, 103–5
   jewel (*Ludisia discolor*), 103
   lady's slipper (*Paphiopedilum* spp.
     and cvs.), 47, 103, *104,* 133
   masdevallia, *10*
   moth (*Phalaenopsis* spp.), 105
outdoor uses for terrariums, *126,*
   130–33, *132,* 137
overgrown plants, 78–79, 100

palms, 74
paphiopedilum orchids, 47, 103,
   104, 133
papyrus, *106,* 107
paths, 66, 149
peacock moss, *102*
peat moss, 66
pebbles or gravel, 66–67, *67,* 68, *70,*
   145, 149
pelargoniums, 122
Pellaea rotundifolia, 96
Pennisetum setaceum, 105
peperomias, *14,* 37, 43, 107–10, *108,*
   109, 127
perennials, 25–26, 130
Persian shield, 110
phalaenopsis orchids, 105
piggyback plant, 122–23, *123*
pileas, 28, 110–12, *120*
   creeping Charlie, *111,* 112, *155*

pinecones, 11, *101*
pitcher plants, 90, *92, 93*
planting terrariums, 70–71
 case studies, 161–67
plants, 20–29
 choosing, 23, 55–59
 collections of, 141–42
 design principles and, 61–66
 humidity-loving, 55, 122
 miniature, 55, 56
 perennials, 25–26
 root systems of, 56–59, 70–71
 shade-loving, 55, 84
 that won't grow in terrariums, 122
 wild, 24, 26, 100
 see also specific plants
plastic terrariums, 27, 52
polypodiums, *59*, 94–96
porches, 50, 52, 130
potted plants, *10, 14, 18, 22, 25–27, 37, 38, 54, 60, 61, 84, 85, 87, 91, 95, 108, 109, 121, 128, 131, 154, 155*
 putting into jar, aquarium, or case, 163–64
prayer plants, 119
princess pine, 24, *80*
propagating plants:
 rooting cuttings, *133, 155*, 155–56, *156*, 167–68
 starting seeds, *46, 133*, 134

quarantining infested plants, 80–81

radiators, 50, *94, 106*, 138
recuperating plants, terrariums for, 157–58
red spider mites, 81
rooting cuttings, *133, 155*, 155–56, *156*, 167–68
root systems, 56–59, 70–71
rotating terrariums toward light, 65, 79
rush, common, *106*

Sagina subulata, 120
saintpaulias (African violets), 23, 27, *98*, 99
sand, 66, 68, 145
Sarracenia spp. (pitcher plants), 90, *92, 93*
saucers, *54*
Saxifraga spp., *85*, 120–21
scale, 81

scillas, 129
seashells, 11, 22, 32, *131*, 145, *145*
sedges, 105, 107
seeds, starting, *46, 133*, 134
selaginellas, 100–102, *101, 102*
sensitive plant, 113
Serissa foetida, 121
shade-loving plants, 55, 84
shape, design and, 61–62
silver squill, *118*, 119
Sinningia pusilla, 99
slugs, 81
snails, 81
snowdrops, 29, *58*, 129
snow rose, 121
soil, 66, *67*, 70
 planting in, 70–71, 162
 testing consistency of, 66, *68*
 testing moisture content of, 76
Soleirolia soleirolli (baby's tears), *51*, 120, 121
Solenostemon scutellaroides (coleus), 121, *121*, 137, 156
sphagnum moss, 66, 68
spring, terrariums in, 126–29, *128*
spring bulbs, 25, 126, *128*, 129
 snowdrops, 29, *58*, 129
starfish, *143*, 145
stones, 11, 16, 145, *146, 147*
 see also pebbles or gravel
strawberry geranium, 120–21
Streptocarpus cvs., *97*, 99
stressed plants, 81, 157–58
succulents, 55, 122
summer, terrariums in, 130–34, *131*
sundew, 90, 93
sunlight:
 outdoor use of cloches and, 130–33
 seasonal variations in, 27, 138
 windows and, 27, 52
 see also light
supermarket houseplants, 23

teddy bear vine, 115
temperature fluctuations, 50, 52
temporary terrarium installations, 50, 55, 133–34
test tubes, 19, 46
Tetranema roseum, 122
textures, design and, 61, 62, *64*
thick glass, *48*
threes, planting in, 62–65
tillandsias, *8, 89*, 89–90, *141*
Tolmiea menziesii, 122–23, *123*

tools, 66–69, *67*
toys, *69, 127, 139, 153, 159*
tropical plants, 40
 see also orchids
trowels, 68
tureens, *45*, 46, 60–61, *84, 144*
twigs, *12, 124, 145*

umbrella plant (*Cyperus* spp.), *106*, 107
urns, 62

vacations:
 mementos from, 143–45, *143–45, 147*
 terrarium use during, 134
vases, *10, 19*, 20, 46, *47*, 60–61, 76, 89, *106, 111, 143*
ventilation, 20, 46, 60–61, 138
 outdoor terrariums and, 130–33
 raising cloches on "feet" for, 60, *78, 123*, 133
 Wardian cases and, 43, 60
Venus flytrap, 90–93
violets (violas), *82*, 84, 123, *123*
vistas, design principles and, 66

Ward, Nathaniel, 40, 93, 96
Wardian cases, *17, 21*, 40–43, *41, 42*, 56, *57*, 60, 61, *64, 72, 74, 86, 93, 114, 121, 146, 148, 149, 151, 152*
 planting in, 163, 165–67
 ventilation and, 43, 60
 watering plants in, 60, *60*, 75
washing terrariums, 70, *75*, 79, 81
watering, 29, 71, *75*, 75–76, 134, 138, 158
 judging moisture in soil and, 75, 76, *77*
 ventilation and, 78
 Wardian cases, 60, *60*, 75
wildflowers and other wild plants, 24, 26, 100, *152*
wilting, 74, 75, 78
windows, 27, 52
 see also light
winter, terrariums in, 138–40, *139*
winterberry, *140*
wood hyacinth, *128*, 129
work, terrarium as calling-card for, 124
workplaces, terrariums in, *11, 12*, 27, *27, 84*, 124